GREEN BAY
MURDER & MAYHEM

TIMOTHY FREISS

THE
History
PRESS

Published by The History Press
Charleston, SC
www.historypress.com

Front cover, top left: Federal Bureau of Investigation; *top center*: Wikimedia Commons; *top right*: Encyclopedia Titanica; *bottom*: Getty Images.
Back cover: Evan Freiss.

First published 2023

Manufactured in the United States

ISBN 9781467153690

Library of Congress Control Number: 2023937202

*I would like to dedicate this book to my wife, Cherri,
and to my children, Trevor, McKenna, Evan and Meredith.
I also want to thank my parents, Mae and Ken, whom I miss very much.*

CONTENTS

ACKNOWLEDGEMENTS

I want to thank my daughter McKenna and my son Evan for their help in putting this book together.

—Tim Freiss

INTRODUCTION

Green Bay is best known for America's favorite football team, the Green Bay Packers. It's also known for its midwestern charm and for having a community of hardworking, friendly and generous people. Though it has a population of over 102,000 and is the third-largest city in Wisconsin, many feel that Green Bay has the security of a small town, the sort of place where "nothing ever happens."

But Green Bay has an underlying wickedness to it that has been there from its formation. For instance, did you know that its downtown district was built on top of one of Wisconsin's oldest burial sites? Green Bay's west side was the location for the state's second recorded hanging, the method at the time to execute those convicted of murder. And the city's beloved football team, the Packers, once drafted one of America's worst serial killers.

No matter your thoughts or opinions about Green Bay, after reading this book, you will likely see this homey town a little differently.

1

THE 1931 ROBBERY OF
THE SOUTH SIDE STATE BANK

T he 1920s and 1930s proved to be a wild time in American history. Both the Great Depression and Prohibition had people desperate and on the edge. Gangsters such as the infamous bank robber John Dillinger and the bootlegger* Al Capone were making their names known at this time, and Hollywood was eager to exploit this racketeering lifestyle in film. Golden age actors like James Cagney and Edward G. Robinson made a career of portraying romanticized versions of these outlaws on the screen.

While Hollywood was inspired by these crimes, Green Bay's Southside State Bank would feel the sting of such gangsters' influence.

On July 20, 1931, the Green Bay Police Department received two calls informing it of a possible bank robbery. The first call came from A.W. Juster. Juster worked at a printing shop located directly across the street from the Southside State Bank. He claimed to have seen three gunmen run into the bank, with another two standing guard outside. Almost immediately after the call from Juster ended, the phone began to ring yet again. This time, the call came from a man named Paul M. Clifford, a dentist who was renting a space directly above the bank. He stated that the bank had been robbed, which led police to believe that the robbery was already finished. After all, 99 percent of robberies are over by the time the police arrive.

"If I would have known the robbery was still in progress, the tactical response would have been different," Chief Hawley, who oversaw the

---

* *Bootlegger* was a term used to describe people who illegally produced and distributed alcohol during Prohibition.

operation, later stated. But as it was, the four responding officers—Lieutenant Detective August "Gus" Delloye, Captain Martin Burke, Officer Elmer Denamur and, of course, Chief Hawley himself—were unprepared for what awaited them at the scene.

Denamur, who was the one driving, unknowingly parked the police car directly in front of the gangsters' getaway vehicle. Almost instantly, the two lookout gunmen started shooting at the squad car. With no time to react, Detective Delloye was shot twice, once in his left eye and once in his left forearm. With the injuries rendering him unable to fire, Delloye quickly exited the vehicle and ran to a nearby alley for cover. Captain Burke curled up in a fetal position across the back seat, where he would remain for the duration of the shoot-out. Hawley was hit in the chest by flying pieces of glass from the shattered car window. Denamur was also hit by the glass, but he received only a minor scratch on his right cheek.

With only this injury, Denamur returned fire. He successfully struck one of the gangsters in his right shoulder. The gangster, no longer able to shoot, fled north on Broadway toward West Mason Street. From here, the fleeing man was spotted by several witnesses.

At 11:16 a.m., a Mrs. Henry Huth saw the wounded bandit run down an alleyway past her house. He then ran north on Maple. She stated that he was of medium build and wearing a reddish-brown suit and a straw hat.

At 11:20 a.m., Al Degroot of Degroot and Allen Electric saw a dark Nash sedan speeding north on Twelfth (just west of Ashland). He stated that he saw one man in the front of the car and two others in the back seat. The car allegedly bore an Illinois license plate, the first two numbers being 48.

Lloyd Delarvelle, a Green Bay citizen who was driving along West Mason Street, also spotted the injured gangster. At first, he considered running him over with his car. But he ultimately decided not to when he saw a suspicious black sedan following after the man. He figured this car was full of more armed gangsters, so he decided to turn around and drive away.

At 11:23 a.m., Frank Garhusky, a mechanic at Pankratz Motor Car Company, allegedly saw the gangsters as they left the bank. He claimed they were driving a maroon 1929 Studebaker President sedan with a trunk in the back.

At 11:25 a.m., Mrs. George Vandenboom saw two cars speeding down Maple Avenue. She saw the wounded bandit picked up by the maroon car, with a blue Nash following close behind. A Mr. Longvist, another witness to this, said he could see blood streaming down the right elbow of the man as he entered the car.

Police followed this literal blood trail left by the gangster, but it eventually went cold. Unfortunately, DNA testing was not in existence at this time, so the blood the gangster left behind was of no help.

The total operation took about thirty-two minutes. About $7,000 was stolen (roughly $113,250 today). After the bank robbers fled, Hawley, Delloye and Denamur were brought to local hospitals for treatment of their wounds. Hawley's and Denamur's injuries were minor, and they went back to work that same day. Burke, having sustained no injuries, continued to be lead investigator on the case. Detective Delloye, on the other hand, was in critical condition. The bullet that had penetrated his left eye was lodged in his skull; removal would be deadly. In the long run, it was decided to leave the bullet in rather than attempt to remove it. Delloye's eye could not be saved, and he used a glass eye for the rest of his life. Thankfully, no major arteries were damaged in his left arm, and it healed on its own.

Delloye returned to duty on September 1, 1931. But because of his disability, he could no longer serve as a detective and was reassigned to a night shift commander position. The city council determined that since Delloye was 25 percent disabled, he should receive just 75 percent of his salary. Delloye took the city to court over this and won the case, but the city still refused to pay him his full salary.

Only two people were hurt inside the bank during the robbery. One was an assistant cashier named Frank Slupinski. He had been ordered by a gunman to open the vault. After it was opened, the gangster was disappointed by the amount of cash inside. He took his anger out on Slupinski and started to kick and beat the man as he repeatedly asked where the securities and gold were kept. Other gunmen joined in, beating Slupinski in the face with the wooden butts of their tommy guns, crushing his nose, deviating his septum, crushing his cheekbones and lacerating his face. At some point during the beating, Slupinski became unconscious. Cayer, a fellow employee, attempted to stop the vicious attack on his coworker, but the gangsters turned on him, and he was also beaten unconscious. Both men survived their injuries.

Mugshot of John Dillinger. *Federal Bureau of Investigation.*

As for the gangsters, due to limited evidence, they were never caught. But several theories emerged in the community about who committed the crime.

The most prominent theory was that the robbery had been organized by John Dillinger. This theory was largely based on the facts that the Southside gangsters seemed experienced and the robbery was executed in Dillinger's signature style.

One of the reasons for the connection to Dillinger was that the Southside Bank Robbery gangsters were reported to be wearing suits. One of the most well-known traits of Dillinger and his gang was that they wore suits during their stickups. This was done in an attempt to mimic the appearance of businessmen so as not to raise suspicion. It is from Dillinger and his gang that we get the stereotype of gangsters in suits and ties.

Another element of the robbery similar to Dillinger's crimes was the fact that each of the bank robbers seemed to have an assigned role. Dillinger was known to assign particular duties to members of his gang during stickups.

Lastly, and perhaps most convincingly, it was reported that one of Dillinger's girlfriends actually lived in Green Bay at the time and worked at a building only a few blocks from the bank. Rumors circulated that Dillinger had been visiting her during the time of the robbery. This proved to be false, as Dillinger was later found to be incarcerated at the time and had no way of committing the crime.

Another theory surfaced after the Kraft Bank in Menominee, Wisconsin, was robbed on October 20 of that year. People speculated that the robbers were the same as those from Southside Bank. This robbery also had a Dillinger style to it, leading to the potential connection. But none of the eyewitness descriptions of these robbers matched those at Southside. One of the Southside State Bank gangsters was said to be five feet tall with a medium build and with a dark complexion that made him look Italian. No suspect at the Kraft robbery matched this specific description.

A man named John Frawley later came forward with the claim that he knew who had committed the Southside robbery. But after a short investigation into his claim, it was determined that Frawley wasn't a very credible source and was believed to have only said it for notoriety.

A vehicle that matched the Southside gangsters'—a Nash car*—was spotted in a wooded area off of Taylor Street. When a posse† approached the suspicious vehicle, the owners took off running. It was later revealed

* Funnily enough, Nash automobiles were produced in Kenosha, Wisconsin, and were famous for being the preferred car of gangsters of the time because of their spaciousness. This allowed for the mounting of a tripod or turret on the floor, on which the gangsters could place their tommy guns, giving them 360-degree firepower. The dashboard could also be mounted with a swivel packet for placement of a tommy gun.

† A group of people, typically vigilantes, who went after criminals.

Police officer in front of a call box, 1912. *Library of Congress, Prints and Photographs Division.*

that the owners were just a couple of bootleggers attempting to carry off a barrel of beer.

A witness phoned in a tip that the gangsters supposedly used a covered truck to conceal themselves when they escaped. The last reported possible sighting of them was on July 28, 1931, at a filling station in New Holstein, Wisconsin, about forty-five miles to the south of Green Bay. Two of the men appeared injured, and a woman was supposedly driving the car. Nothing else ever came up, and the identity of those who organized the crime remains a mystery.

Interesting Sidenote

In 1931, the Green Bay Police Department (GBPD) consisted of only three squad cars and thirty-six sworn officers. The primary means of patrol was on foot, and officers, without radios, had to walk to call boxes to receive their assigned duties. Calls were sometimes left unanswered if no officer was nearby. In the event of an emergency, all call boxes would ring and motor vehicle officers would respond. This was a time before the institution of 911 as an emergency phone number. To reach the police department, one dialed Adam 87. This proved difficult both to remember and to dial under the stress of an emergency, hence the change to 911.

2

ROBERT E. MINAHAN

ONE OF THE BRAVEST MAYORS
TO EVER SERVE THE CITY OF GREEN BAY

Born on January 27, 1858, Robert E. Minahan was the oldest son of seven children. His parents, Mary and William Minahan, were Irish immigrants who moved to Howard, New York, where they worked as farmers. Two years after Robert was born, the family moved up to Calumet County, Wisconsin, where Robert would spend the rest of his childhood.

After he graduated from the Oshkosh public school system, he enrolled at Oshkosh State Normal School, a teacher training facility (now the University of Wisconsin–Oshkosh). In 1880, he graduated and subsequently became a teacher in Cedarburg, Wisconsin. On December 28 of that year, he married Ellen "Nellie" Mulcahy. He and Ellen had met as kids when Robert lived in Calumet County, and the two rekindled their friendship as adults. They went on to have one son together, Eben Roger Minahan.*

In 1882, Robert, Ellen and his brother John moved to Chicago, where Robert attended Rush Medical College. John supported his brother's education through the money he made working as a streetcar operator. After Robert earned his MD in 1886, he returned to his childhood home in Calumet Harbor, Wisconsin. It was there that he began to practice medicine. Around this same time, he returned the favor to his brother, supporting John financially while he attended Rush Medical College.

After six years of practicing medicine, in 1892, Robert decided he wanted to go back to school. This time he chose to study law at the University of

---

* Later on, Eben became a successful lawyer, but he would live only to the age of forty-six, dying of meningitis in 1928.

Michigan. After passing his bar exam in 1894, he started practicing law in Kewaunee, Wisconsin. He stayed there for three years until 1898, when he moved to Green Bay. Once there, he and John practiced medicine at the St. Vincent Hospital, in addition to practicing law.

Six years went by, after which Robert yet again decided he wanted a change of career. This time, he ran for mayor of Green Bay in 1904. At the time of Robert's campaign, Green Bay was a bit of a seedy place. It had its fair share of corruption and hosted several illegal gambling establishments. Robert vowed that he would take care of these problems once and for all should he be elected. His campaign was successful. Robert won the election in a landslide. It was said to be the largest winning margin ever seen in a Green Bay mayoral race for its time.

Robert wasted no time fulfilling his promise. After only two months in office, he went to work on cleaning up Green Bay. He started with hiring several crews of men to go out collecting all the illegal gambling devices in the city. He instructed the crews to be gentle with these removals and to not damage the machines, in an attempt to avoid any conflict with the machines' owners. This seemed to work. None of the owners protested the removal of the machines. After all, they had prior experience with mayors removing their gambling devices, after which they simply paid a fine and had the machines returned. They figured this time would be like those previous instances.

They could not have been more wrong. Once the collection was complete, the gambling devices were brought back to City Hall, where they were dumped onto the front lawn. Robert exited City Hall, his sleeves rolled up,

Robert E. Minahan's grave as it looks today. *Evan Freiss.*

with a sledgehammer in one hand and an axe in the other. In a shocking scene, the newly elected mayor began to smash the devices to bits. For added measure, he poured kerosene over the pile and burned the devices to ashes.

Spectators of this scene were in awe of his bravery. But Robert wouldn't get away with this act scot-free. For the next few months, he received multiple death threats, requiring extra security for a significant time afterward. But no attempt was ever made on his life.

This act alone would be a crowning achievement for any mayor, but Robert didn't intend to stop there. Before he left office, he asked for the resignation and removal of both the fire chief, William Kennedy, and police officer and Detective Captain William E. Finnegan, both on charges of extortion and bribery.

Finnegan had a history of taking money for performing police duties. The main case against him was from citizen Thomas R. Haverty. On February 22, 1907, Haverty had gone to Finnegan for help with a personal issue. Finnegan agreed to take the case, but only for a fee of $100 (roughly $2,817 today). The reason for the fee, Finnegan claimed, was to cover the cost of services he was providing as a "private" detective. This was not the first time Finnegan had done something like this.

When Finnegan was confronted about these misdemeanors, his defense was that he was on vacation when he worked on the cases. Therefore, he was off duty and performing the investigative work on his own time and with his own money. He argued that he should be compensated. But Finnegan was salaried, and he was accepting these cases without clearing them with the Green Bay Police Department. He resigned on March 15, 1907.

As for the fire chief, William Kennedy, he was caught accepting a bribe from a man by the name of Charles E. Johnson. The bribe was $100 and was to secure a contract with the Seagrave Company, ensuring that the Green Bay Fire Department would purchase any equipment it needed through them. He pleaded guilty to charges of bribery and was officially relieved of his duties as fire chief on May 11, 1906. Mayor Robert Minahan stated that Kennedy's actions had betrayed and grossly misrepresented the confidence of the people of Green Bay.

After his time as mayor was over, Robert went on to be a bank executive. He later returned to practicing medicine. He became known as one of the top surgeons in the area. Dr. Robert E. Minahan lived to the age of seventy-seven, dying peacefully in his home on April 27, 1935. His younger brother, William Minahan, experienced a much more dramatic death. We will touch on this later.

3
MURDER AT THE GOLDEN PHEASANT

The murder at the Golden Pheasant is still considered one of Green Bay's most brutal and grotesque crimes. But before it became the site of a horrific act, the Golden Pheasant was known for something entirely different.

The Golden Pheasant owed its popularity not to its delicious hamburgers and fried chicken but to something more nefarious on the menu. It was a popular speakeasy* during Prohibition. It was a place where patrons could purchase bootleg liquor. There were also several illegal quarter and dime slot machines that patrons could play while they drank.

The Golden Pheasant's owner was Jack Van Veghel, who also went by the name of John. Jack was known to the community as a well-respected and endeared member, said to be very giving and caring. But Jack hadn't had an easy life prior to starting his business. At the young age of twenty-two, he experienced immense heartbreak, losing both his wife and his infant daughter to the flu epidemic of 1916. It was after this tragic incident that Van Veghel decided to devote all his attention to business, perhaps as a way to distract himself.

He first started Van's Saloon, which was located at the northeast corner of George and Main Streets. Later, Jack moved the business to Willow Street and renamed it the Golden Pheasant. Following the success of this business,

_____

* A place where alcoholic beverages are illegally sold, specifically a place during Prohibition in the United States.

he helped his brother establish what was known at the time as a "soft drink" saloon. In reality, it was also a place where patrons could get a much stronger beverage than a soft drink—for the right price.

Working as a waitress and a cook at the Golden Pheasant was a twenty-four-year-old woman by the name of Lucille Birdsall, who had only just moved to Green Bay. After her divorce, she and her young daughter, Betty Jane, moved from Milwaukee to live with her parents in their home in Sturgeon Bay. Eventually, Birdsall decided she was ready to try to make it on her own and moved to Green Bay. At the Golden Pheasant, she made her presence known to the community and was said to be a hardworking, fun-loving and well-liked woman. Unbeknownst to the community, however, Jack (who was thirty-six at the time) and Lucille had entered into a relationship.

On Monday, May 19, 1930, something unusual happened. Mrs. William Debroux, a neighbor of the Golden Pheasant, noticed that the business hadn't been opened all day and became increasingly concerned. She also noticed that Jack's gray 1929 Chevrolet car was parked out front, which implied that he was in the building. Yet when the baker, the iceman, the public service meter reader and the milkman all came to the roadhouse, no one answered the door. Mrs. Debroux began to worry that there might be a gas leak and that Jack and Lucille had asphyxiated. She asked her husband to go next door and smell for gas. He found nothing of the sort and decided not to investigate any further.

But when Mrs. Debroux woke the next morning, the Golden Pheasant still wasn't open. Becoming even more worried, she decided to send her young son Martin, ten, to investigate. Climbing on top of an old streetcar that was being used as storage, Martin peeked into the upper window of Jack Van Veghel's bedroom. On that Tuesday, May 20, at 5:20 a.m., Martin discovered the bodies of a violent murder. What he saw was a scene so gruesome, it would horrify anyone, especially a child. Extremely upset, Martin ran home crying and returned to his mother hysterical. He said that he saw blood splattered everywhere and two people butchered like "the way grandpa slaughters chickens."

The news of this murder quickly spread. By 7:00 a.m. that Tuesday morning, only an hour and a half after the bodies had been discovered, more than one hundred people had gathered outside of the Golden Pheasant. Dozens of looters had reached the scene before the police, breaking in and taking souvenirs from the restaurant. This completely contaminated the crime scene and made fingerprinting impossible.

The bodies were confirmed to be those of Jack Van Veghel and Lucille Birdsall. Police later determined that sometime between 4:00 a.m. and 6:00 a.m. the prior morning, May 19, Van Veghel and Birdsall were hacked to death in their bed. The murder weapon was believed to be a hatchet. Jack had received multiple deep gashes to his face and head. It was said that the wounds were so severe they resembled the destructive blast of a shotgun. He appeared to have been the first victim of the attack, and it was possible that he never fully woke from his sleep to realize the horror of what was happening to him. Lucille on the other hand appeared to have fought back. There were wounds on her body that suggested a horrendous struggle. Her right forearm had been sliced several times to the bone. Her face and neck had also received several deep slashes.

During the investigation, deputies found that two slot machines had been smashed open. At the time of the murder, there had recently been a string of burglaries in the area involving slot machines. At first, police considered the idea that the murders were one of those robberies gone wrong. In fact, Jack's family was convinced that this theory was the only possible explanation for the murders. As stated earlier, Jack was a well-loved member of the community and had no known enemies. Police began to speculate that the destruction of the slot machines could have happened after the murders. It is possible that, after seeing there was no activity in the business that Monday, thieves took advantage of the situation and attempted a quick theft, so the police did not investigate further.

Interestingly, this theory actually had a positive effect on the community. The rumors of a burglary gone wrong quickly spread; as a result, there were no burglaries or slot machine thefts in the area for quite some time after. It seemed as though no burglars wanted to take the chance of being associated with the double homicide.

The first official suspect to be considered for the crime was Lucille Birdsall's ex-husband, Frank Kupsack, even though he lived in Milwaukee at the time of the murder. After hearing about the death of his ex-wife, Frank voluntarily drove up to Green Bay to be arrested, figuring that he would be the primary suspect due to his and Lucille's rocky relationship. He was fully compliant with the police, stating that he just wanted to help bring the murderer of his child's mother to justice.

However, when deputies investigated the Golden Pheasant's basement, they discovered a lathe installer's hatchet with blood all over it. Kupsack worked as a lathe installer by trade and did actually own a hatchet, but he claimed to have left it at his home in Milwaukee. Despite this seemingly

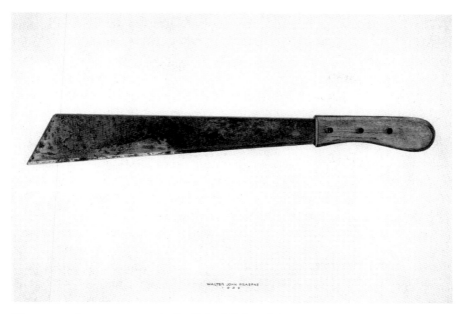

The suspected weapon: a corn knife. *National Gallery of Art.*

damning evidence, Kupsack was eventually cleared of the charges. The first evidence of Kupsack's innocence came from Irene Clowry, a waitress at the Golden Pheasant. She was asked to identify Kupsack, as she had recalled that a couple of different men had recently been in the Pheasant to see Lucille. But Kupsack was not identified as one of them. Later, after forensic investigation, it was determined that the discovered hatchet was actually covered in chicken blood, not the blood of Lucille and Jack. After this, Kupsack was released from jail and pardoned from any charges.

Another suspect was a convict named Thomas Donnelly (also known under the alias Jim McGilth). His cellmate, a man named W.G. Foss, said that Donnelly claimed that Lucille Birdsall had been his girlfriend. More shockingly, Foss stated that Donnelly had confessed of the murders to him. Prior to Foss's claim, both Foss and Donnelly had been caught trying to escape the jail together, and it was only after this that Foss made these statements. Specifically, he claimed that Donnelly was trying to escape because he was fearful of being brought up on murder charges, and Foss said he had been roped into Donnelly's plan. Therefore, it is likely that Foss's claims were only to protect himself. With no other evidence, and with Donnelly denying the claims himself, Donnelly was never brought up on the charges.

The murder weapon was never found, and no one was ever brought up on the charges. In 1990, sixty years after the murders, David Ray, a psychic from Neenah, Wisconsin, conducted a séance at what once was the Golden Pheasant. Ray used a technique known as automatic writing, in which he allowed spirits to come through to him and write whatever it is they wanted to say. He claimed that he managed to connect and communicate with the spirit of Lucille. She allegedly told him that the weapon the killer used was not a hatchet but a corn knife. Lucille also told him that the killer had died in 1940, a decade after the murders, in a car crash.

The Golden Pheasant was torn down quite some time ago. It was once located at 2015 Willow Street and was in the town of Preble. Now, this area is part of Green Bay's far east side, and the spot where the Golden Pheasant stood is now (at the time of this writing) a strip mall located at 2247 University Avenue. The case still remains a mystery and likely always will.

4
GRAVE BEGINNINGS

I t's hard to imagine that someone would intentionally desecrate the final resting places of hundreds of people. Unfortunately, that is exactly what happened to one of Wisconsin's oldest burial sites. What you may know today as Green Bay's downtown district was once home to the departed.

Long before the first white settlers set foot in Wisconsin, the area was a Native American burial ground, used primarily by Wisconsin's local Menominee and Winnebago tribes (and occasionally the nonlocal Fox and Sauk tribes). In 1740, the first French settlers entered Green Bay, and they too used these burial grounds for their people. They named this land the La Baye Burial Place. The English settlers also used the graveyard for their dead, and when the first permanent settlers moved here, they used it as well, until its closure in 1838.

The graveyard would be the resting place for numerous key figures of the time. Several prominent family members of the Potawatomie, Menominee, Ojibwa, Ho-Chunk, Miami, Sauk and Fox tribes were buried on these grounds. It was also home to some of the French nobility who died here during the war in 1733. Wisconsin's first permanent resident, dubbed the "father of Wisconsin," soldier and fur trader Charles Michel Langlade, was among the graveyard's inhabitants. And the graveyard was also the final resting place for Kinanotamn, the daughter of the Menominee chief, and her husband, Joseph Leroy. Leroy was a French settler and builder who actually erected the oldest standing structure in the state (which you can find

Downtown Green Bay. *Evan Freiss*.

presently at Heritage Hill, Green Bay's Historical State Park). But despite the historical and spiritual value of the land, the La Baye Burial Place inevitably fell victim to progress and growth. The perpetuators were two men, both named John Jacob Astor.

The first John Jacob Astor was a shrewd and ruthless businessman who became the nation's first reported millionaire. He made his first million in the importing and exporting business. His biggest and most profitable product was opium, which he exported from Africa and brought to both China and the United States. After several decades in this business, Astor, perhaps growing nostalgic for his days as a young man working as a fur trader, decided to change career paths. He went on to start his own fur-trading establishment, the American Fur Trade Company.

Astor had made numerous connections in politics over the years, and he used this to his advantage. He petitioned for a law that would make it illegal for anyone to do business with fur trappers located outside of the United States. While this appears to be a positive action at face value, Wisconsin wasn't a legal part of the United States at this time, making it a foreign entity. In turn, the trappers here were no longer able to do business with

Left: Portrait of John Jacob Astor, 1794, by Gilbert Stuart. Brook Club, New York. *Wikimedia Commons*.

Right: John Jacob Astor IV. *Wikimedia Commons*.

their U.S. counterparts. Wisconsin (namely, Green Bay) was known for its fur-trapping industry, so this policy disrupted the livelihoods of the majority of people living here at the time.

Astor, now having control over most of the fur-trading business in the country, decided to extend a helping hand and offer these Wisconsin fur trappers a deal they couldn't refuse. He offered to purchase their properties. In return, they would come to New York and work for the American Fur Trade Company. He would also provide housing and food for them and their families. Having little choice at this point, given that most were now out of work and in poverty, most of the workers agreed to his proposition. As a result, Astor wound up owning most of Green Bay, including the La Baye Burial Place. Meanwhile, the workers who agreed to the deal found very poor working conditions. Astor deducted the cost of housing and food from their wages, which meant they were paid almost nothing for their labor.

For decades, the La Baye Burial Place remained in Astor's name until it eventually fell into the possession of his great-grandson John Jacob Astor IV. The younger Astor was just as conniving as his great-grandfather and saw in the burial site a budding opportunity. Astor viewed the burial place as a waste of landscape and thought the graveyard would be the perfect place to build the first waterworks plant in Green Bay.

Astor started the construction by hiring crews of men to remove the tombstones. Where exactly all of the tombstones disappeared to is uncertain, but it has been discovered that some were thrown into the Fox River. Over the years, even as recently as this past decade, some people have reported finding waterworn tombstones washed up on the Fox River shore, the engravings so eroded that the stones are only recognizable by their distinctive tombstone shapes.

With the tombstones gone, the next step was to figure out what to do with the bodies. It was reported that during the development of the waterworks several bodies were unearthed to make room for the placement of the water mains. The remains were tossed with the common dirt, without any care or concern.

Several citizens witnessed this vile behavior and decided to confront Astor about it. But their concerns were ignored. Astor told them that if they wanted him to stop, they would have to get the mayor to come down himself and tell him personally. But Astor knew full well that the mayor would do

The Fox River. *Evan Freiss.*

no such thing. Not only was the waterworks plant a great opportunity for the town, the mayor (as well as several other prominent and wealthy figures in the community) also had personally invested in the project. Having little luck with legal tactics, the citizens attempted to appeal to Astor's spiritual side. They brought in a local priest in the hopes of guilting Astor to stop. But Astor replied in the same condescending manner. The only way he would stop was if the mayor was on their side. Without that, there was no way to stop the desecration.

At that time, the local Catholic diocese became involved, supplying several boxes for transportation of the recovered remains. Some of the bodies were reburied in a mass grave at the cemetery east of St. John, at the Evangelist Catholic Church in Shantytown, now known as the Allouez Catholic Cemetery. The mass grave for a time was unmarked, though it is possible that a marker did exist at one point and simply rotted away over time. It would be rediscovered only in 1931, when a cemetery worker, while digging a trench, unearthed the twenty-foot-long ditch filled with decayed human remains. The mass grave can still be found there today, in lots 312–13 of section AA North. It is believed that other remains were relocated to what is now Baird Place, at the corner of West Mason Street and South Webster Avenue. Some remains were left behind, resting beneath what is now the streets of downtown Green Bay.

Over the decades, human remains have continued to be dug up around the Downtown Green Bay area. In fact, the unearthing of bodies became so frequent that most places located downtown are not allowed to build basements so as not to disrupt anything that might be buried beneath. Most recently, in April 2006, human remains were once again uncovered during work along South Adams Street. Wisconsin statute states that, when found, human remains must be carefully replaced in the area where they were discovered. So, in this case, the bodies were quietly put back.

The exact dimensions of the burial place are still unknown. Unlike other graveyards in Green Bay, La Baye was abandoned and erased from city maps. But the placement of bodies discovered over the years has been helpful in determining the rough location. Presently, we can place it underneath several streets, from Washington to Adams and from Crooks to Chicago. But it is believed that the graveyard is much larger than this. This raises a question: How many more bodies are still to be discovered underneath Green Bay?

The La Baye Historical Research Committee, along with the mayor's beautification committee, have been attempting to establish a fund to

Allouez Catholic Cemetery and Chapel Mausoleum. *Evan Freiss.*

purchase some of the land on the graveyard's site. The hope is to eventually set up a monument in honor of all those who were buried there. The monument would list the names of all known persons whose final resting places had at one time been the La Baye Burial Place.

John Astor IV, after creating the first waterworks in Green Bay, would ironically die by water. He was one of the passengers who drowned on the *Titanic*. Some say that this is a fitting payback for his destruction of Wisconsin's oldest burial grounds.

LA BAYE BURIAL PLACE

It should be noted that La Baye Burial Place is more appropriately referred to as a graveyard or a burial place rather than a cemetery. This is because cemeteries were developed later, during the Victorian era. They were landscaped plots generally found on the outskirts of town, often prettied up with tree-lined pathways and ornate borders. In fact, they were so pretty that people often held picnics and did daily walks through cemeteries, as this was a time before parks existed. This actually inspired the development of two industries or trades: architectural landscaping (people wanted to have their lawns resemble the nature of these "garden cemeteries") and park development (people wanted to have scenic places to visit, without tombstones). Graveyards and burial places, however, were purely functional, serving as undecorated repositories for bodies and often located within a city and near a church.

5

ELEAZER WILLIAMS

THE LOST DAUPHIN

One of the greatest mysteries in European history is the fate of the son of Queen Marie Antoinette and King Louis XVI. Dubbed the "Lost Dauphin," Louis-Charles was set to be the heir to the throne of France, but he never received that title. His fate was a centuries-long mystery that somehow found its way to Green Bay, Wisconsin.

In 1792, during the French Revolution, King Louis XVI and Queen Marie Antoinette were unseated from their throne. Louis XVI was killed at the guillotine, and his wife and son were held in the Temple Prison in Paris. Marie Antoinette eventually met the same fate as her husband, dying in a public beheading. But Louis-Charles, eight years old at the time, was left in prison. His living conditions were less than humane. He was left in a windowless room for most of this time, and his treatment resembled that of a caged animal. It is believed that he saw almost no one for over six months. After two years of this, he died in prison on June 8, 1795. At the time of his death, his body was covered in scabs and tumors. Official records show that Louis-Charles died of tuberculosis.

It wasn't long after the boy's death that speculation about his fate began. A popular rumor circulated that the boy was actually alive and had been taken from his cell and brought to the United States for safekeeping. A look-alike was left in his place and died in the prison. This rumor grew so popular that in 1814, after the monarchy had been restored to France, several men in both France and the United States came forward and claimed to be the Lost Dauphin. One of these men was Eleazer Williams, who resided in Green Bay, Wisconsin.

No one knows for sure when Eleazer Williams was born. He claimed to have no memory of his life before the age of twelve. What is known, however, is that in 1800, Williams was taken in by relatives in Massachusetts. There, he attended Plymouth College. He then volunteered and served as a scout/spy for the American forces in the War of 1812, serving on the northern border of New York.

After the war, Williams decided to stay in New York and became an Episcopal missionary for the Oneida tribe of upper New York State. He managed to gain the respect of tribal members and successfully converted several of them to the Christian faith. He also worked to translate the Episcopal prayer book and hymns into

Portrait of Eleazer Williams by monogrammist Richardson Cox. Putnam's Monthly Magazine *1* *(January–June 1853)*.

the Oneidas' native tongue, the Iroquois language, in revised and simplified Mohawk spelling.

With the continued growth of the country at this time, land agents were eager to claim a stake of the valuable New York Indian reservations. Thomas Ogden, a powerful New York land developer, approached Williams with the proposition of moving several of the Indian tribes—the Stockbridge, Munsee and Oneida—west. This would in turn enable Ogden's company to develop their land. Williams embraced this idea wholeheartedly. He envisioned himself as the spiritual leader of a vast Indian empire in the unsettled Wisconsin wilderness.

The Oneida didn't embrace Williams's vision. Many of them opposed the move to Wisconsin and asked the Episcopal Church to remove Williams as their religious leader. But the church and the War Department both backed Williams, so they had little choice in the matter. In 1822, the first groups of Oneida Indians unwillingly began their long journey to Wisconsin.

Williams led the group with funds supplied by the Ogden Land Company. His hopes were to use this money to purchase land in the Fox River area from the Winnebago and Menominee chiefs. With the help of territorial governor Lewis Cass, Williams persuaded the chiefs to sign a treaty surrendering a four-mile strip of land along the river. In return, the tribes received goods valued at about $3,950. This strip is where they would begin to establish their settlement, at Duck Creek (now known as Howard), located about eight miles northwest of Green Bay.

Shortly after his arrival, Williams worked toward opening a small school in Green Bay for the children of the Indian tribes as well as the white settlers of the area (mainly French fur trappers at this time). The school was a failure and closed only one year after its opening, in 1823. But it was at this school that Williams met fourteen-year-old student Madeline Jordain. The year of the school's closure, Williams married Madeline, despite her being half his age.

Madeline was a descendant of both French fur trappers and Menominee Indians. From her Menominee relatives, she inherited thousands of acres of prime riverfront land, which make up about a third of what is now known as the town of Lawrence. It was on this land that Madeline and Williams built their home, where they would have three children.

Despite his familial obligations, Williams traveled extensively throughout the Midwest in an attempt to persuade new tribes to join his so-called Indian empire. But he found little luck in convincing anyone to agree to take part. So, in 1830, desperate and seeking government support, Williams made his way to Washington, D.C. But instead of Williams receiving help, his plans were callously rejected by government officials.

Feeling defeated and struggling with the growing realization that his dream of an Indian empire had passed, Williams returned to Wisconsin, only to find himself unwanted there as well. He returned to find that the Episcopal Church had replaced him as its missionary. The Oneida had grown tired of his scheming and wanted nothing more to do with him. In his absence, they requested a new missionary. Short on both funds and prospects, Williams abandoned his family in Wisconsin and made his way back to New York.

In 1841, François d'Orléans, Prince de Joinville, the son of the reigning King Louis Philippe of France, was making a tour of the United States. On this journey, he passed through the Great Lakes and, subsequently, Green Bay. The prince, having a fascination with the Oneida tribe, thought this trip would be a great opportunity to learn more about them. It was speculated that the prince knew of Williams serving as the Oneidas' past spiritual leader and actually requested Williams by name. In any case, Williams was to meet with the prince as he passed through the Great Lakes and then accompany him to Green Bay.

Williams eagerly accepted this opportunity. But ever the schemer, he couldn't help but see this as a chance for financial gain. He began to make the claim that he was Louis-Charles, the Lost Dauphin. He knew that being seen roaming around with the prince would add validity to his claim, and thus, more people would be likely to believe it. He later said that the prince had come to Green Bay specifically to see him. Williams told people that the prince was actually there to offer him a vast estate if he would renounce his birthright to the throne.

Eventually, the prince found out about this, and he quickly denied the claim. He said that his only interest in Williams was his background as an Indian missionary. Despite this, the story did not die, and Williams became something of a minor celebrity in the Green Bay area. Influential members of the community paid him to tell stories of his childhood as the prince of France.

After a while, the novelty wore off, and Williams found himself once again broke and unemployed. In 1844, unable to secure steady employment and in financial desperation, he struck a deal with the son of a wealthy New England textile trader, Amos A. Lawrence. Using his wife's tribal land as collateral without her knowledge or consent, Williams took out two loans amounting to over $3,500 (approximately $127,401 today). But Williams's financial

Top: "History of the Dauphin," first published anonymously and later revealed to have been written by Eleazer Williams, 1849. *University of Michigan.*

Bottom: "Have We a Bourbon Among Us?" This article was later revealed to have been written by Eleazer Williams. Putnam's Monthly, *volume 1 (January–June 1853).*

state never improved, and he was unable to buy back his wife's property of five thousand acres from Lawrence. Thankfully, Madeline was allowed to keep her home and continued to live on the land until her death in 1886.

In July 1849, the *United States Magazine and Democratic Review* published an anonymous article boldly stating that Williams's claims were true and that he was indeed the Lost Dauphin. A few years later, in the February 1852 issue of *Putnam's Magazine*, J.H. Hanson, an Episcopal minister, published an article, "Have We a Bourbon Among Us?" The article also supported Williams's claim of being the Lost Dauphin. Despite this brief flurry of attention, Williams remained unsettled and never again reached his highest level of celebrity status. In 1850, he accepted a position to preach to the St. Regis Indians of Hogansberg, New York. He remained there until his death in 1858. After his death, it was revealed that Williams wrote the anonymous article for the *Democratic Review*.

He was originally buried in New York. But in 1947, the Oneida tribe finally forgave Williams of his past actions, and his remains were moved to the Holy Apostle Cemetery in Oneida, on the land he once hoped would be a part of his great Indian empire.

REFERENCES TO ELEAZER WILLIAMS

A mockery of Eleazer Williams's claim to be the lost prince was immortalized in Mark Twain's book *Adventures of Huckleberry Finn*. The book, published in 1884, features a self-described "Lost Dauphin" character that greatly resembles Williams.

In 1937, MGM Studios produced a short film about Williams, *The King without a Crown*, which was shot and premiered in Green Bay.

Several landmarks that reference Williams can be found in the Green Bay area, including Dauphin Street in Allouez, Lost Dauphin Road in the town of Lawrence, Lost Dauphin Park and the Lost Louis Restaurant in Lawrence.

THE LOST PRINCE

Whatever did happen to the lost prince? Though Louis-Charles died, his heart would go on. At the time of the boy's death, a physician named Philippe-Jean Pelletan performed an autopsy. During the autopsy, Pelletan

TRAVELLING BY RAIL.

An illustration from *Adventures of Huckleberry Finn* featuring the King and the Duke, the latter character suspected to be based on Eleazer Williams. E.W. Kemble, 1884. *Wikimedia Commons*.

removed the heart and hid it in a handkerchief. He then brought it home, put it in a jar of alcohol to preserve it and kept it on a shelf as a curiosity. But Pelletan had a loose tongue and couldn't help but confide about the heart to his students. He paid the price for his blabbering when, in 1810, the heart was stolen by one of his students, Jean Henri Tillos.

Ironically, Tillos would contract the same illness as did the late Louis-Charles, tuberculosis, and eventually died from it. But before he did, he confessed his theft to his wife. After his death, his wife returned the heart to Pelletan's family (Pelletan had passed away by this time). Pelletan's wife, unsure of what to do with it, sent the heart to the archbishop of Paris, Hyacinthe-Louis de Quélen. There, the heart was stored in a crystal urn in the Archbishop's Palace of Paris. It remained there for a few years, until 1830, when the palace was raided and the urn smashed. Days later, Pelletan's son went to the palace to look for it and recovered it in a pile of sand. The heart was then sent to the branch of the Bourbon family in Spain.

Opposite, top: Lost Dauphin Road in De Pere, Wisconsin. *Evan Freiss.*

Opposite, bottom: Lost Dauphin State Park in Brown County, Wisconsin. *Evan Freiss.*

Above: Presumed portrait of the Lost Dauphin, the intended King Louis XVII of France. *Jacques Fabien Gautier d'Agoty.*

In 1979, the heart came back to its home in Paris. It was once again put in a crystal vase, but this time, it was kept at the royal crypt in the Basilica of Saint-Denis. In 2000, a DNA test was performed by two separate labs on the heart, comparing its DNA to the hair samples of Marie Antoinette and two of her sisters. It was also compared to the DNA of two living descendants of the royal family. While the tests were not able to identify precisely to whom the heart belonged, they did confirm that it had come from a relative of Marie Antoinette. This meant that the boy who died in prison in 1795 was likely the true Lost Dauphin, Prince Louis-Charles.

In 2004, Louis-Charles finally got to rest in peace instead of in pieces. His heart was removed from its crystal vase and buried alongside the bodies of Louis XVI and Marie Antoinette, and a funeral was held for the boy who would have been King Louis XVII of France.

THE POLICE DETECTIVE WHO MURDERED HIS WIFE—OR DID HE?

The story goes that John Maloney had grown tired of dealing with his estranged wife of nineteen years. She was frequently refusing to attend their divorce hearings, and John, wanting the whole ordeal to be put to rest, decided the best method would be to kill her. And so, on February 10, 1998, John used his background in arson to commit the gruesome murder of Sandy Maloney.

John Maloney and Sandy Cator were high school sweethearts, meeting when they were both attending Preble High School in the late 1970s. In 1979, the summer after graduating, the couple eloped. John later reflected on this time by stating that the first seven years of their marriage were among the happiest times of his life. Sandy was a sweet and loving wife who supported John as he completed his two-year program in criminal justice. After receiving his associate's degree, John became a detective and arson investigator for the Green Bay Police Department, where he worked for the next nineteen years.

Unfortunately, the marriage had begun to deteriorate by the later 1980s. In 1992, Sandy was diagnosed with both panic and generalized anxiety disorders. Her psychologist prescribed the highly addictive drug Klonopin (benzodiazepine). Over the next several years, the woman John had fallen in love with slowly disappeared into prescription drug addiction and alcohol abuse. Her behavior became erratic and unpredictable. On several occasions, she was admitted into rehab programs and mental institutions, but none of this seemed to help. Those closest to her feared that one day she might wind up killing herself.

After several years of this behavior, John couldn't take it anymore. He decided it was finally time for him to move on, and he left Sandy in May 1997. It takes an average of 120 days for a divorce to be finalized in the state of Wisconsin, but John and Sandy's divorce proceedings lasted eight months. Sandy frequently refused to attend scheduled divorce hearings, prolonging the process. Around this time, John started dating a woman who began to put pressure on him to finalize the divorce. On February 10, 1998, John, exasperated and at his wit's end, tried yet again to persuade Sandy to attend a divorce hearing the next morning.

It is unclear whether or not Sandy intended to go, because the following morning, Wednesday, February 11, her charred body was discovered in her house. Sandy's mother was tragically the one who found her. She had come to visit her daughter that morning, and as she entered, she noticed that the house was unusually dark and filled with the smell of smoke. She called out her daughter's name but heard no response. Puzzled by this, Sandy's mother decided to investigate. Entering the living room, she came upon the horrific scene of her daughter's body lying face down on the burned living room sofa.

The original arson reports determined the fire to be accidental. With no suspicious elements or circumstances, the conclusion was that the fire was started by careless cigarette smoking. The autopsy report showed Sandy's blood alcohol content at .36 percent at the time of her death, which is almost four times the legal limit for intoxicated driving and a potentially lethal amount. The autopsy report also discovered bruises on Sandy's neck. This suggested that the manner of death may have been homicide by strangulation. The deputy chief medical examiner listed Sandy's cause of death as "probably manual strangulation." Her death was now considered a homicide case. And John Maloney, having seen her the night before, was the leading suspect.

Sandy, for obvious reasons, failed to show up yet again to the divorce hearing. Though John had been hoping to get custody of his and Sandy's three boys, Sandy's absence meant that nothing could be finalized. After leaving the divorce court, John went back to his sister's house, where she and John's girlfriend were waiting for news of the divorce hearing. The telephone rang, and a detective friend of John's said he was coming over. John hung up the phone and said, as his sister recalled, "Either I really fucked up at work, or Sandy's dead."

Inspecting the crime scene, investigators found five crumpled suicide notes in the kitchen garbage can. They also found an electrical extension cord in the basement that had been tied to a conduit pipe, with one end in the shape of a noose that had failed to hold. Directly beneath the extension cord was a coffee table with two stacked VCRs, which suggested that Sandy had climbed on top of them to reach the noose. Using the blood-detecting chemical luminol, homicide investigators also found blood on the coffee table, in the laundry room, on the floor and in the bathroom. Bloody rags and tissues were found in the trash nearby, and a bloody woman's shirt was found discarded in the laundry hamper. The basement bathroom's shower door revealed even more blood.

Investigators were highly suspicious of John. During their investigation, they employed his girlfriend to try to elicit a confession from him. She had initially been supportive of John, even providing him with an alibi, claiming he was with her the whole night. The only time they were apart was when John went to pick up his son from indoor baseball practice. She agreed to wear a wire only to help prove John's innocence.

But months into the investigation, she began to change her tune. After meeting frequently with investigators, she started to believe that John might actually be guilty of the murder. She even changed their alibi, stating that she did take a nap that night and that it was possible that John snuck out while she was sleeping. Investigators managed to convince her to secretly videotape John visiting her while she was staying in Las Vegas. They even coached her on how to interrogate John about his involvement in Sandy's death.

The resulting video depicts an exasperated John and his girlfriend arguing starting at around 4:49 a.m. She repeatedly insinuates that John murdered Sandy, and John continues to deny it, growing angrier. The heated arguing goes on for most of the entire eighteen-hour tape. She does manage to get John to confess that he was at Sandy's house the night of her death, but only to see if she would show up to the divorce hearing the next day. This was the most damning evidence against John and was used against him in his prosecution. The following is the transcript of that confession, taken directly from the tape.

John's girlfriend: "Did you go there to do it?"
John: "No."
John's girlfriend: "Why did you go there then?..."
John: "To get done with the divorce. To get it over with."

Prosecutor Joseph Paulus used this statement as evidence of John's guilt, stating: "This guy admitted on videotape that he was in the house that night, and that means he did it. The whole case was the videotape....If the videotape hadn't gotten in, we may not have charged the case."

John chose not to testify in his trial. It lasted for eight days and ended on February 17, 1999, almost a year to the day of Sandy's death. The jury was out for twelve hours and came back with a verdict of guilty of first-degree intentional homicide, arson and mutilation of a corpse. John was sentenced to life in prison.

But some facts suggest that John may not be as guilty as he seems. First, key evidence was conveniently omitted from the trial, and the jury never heard other theories regarding possible causes of Sandy's death. One of these theories was that her death was the result of an accidental suicide. Some speculate that Sandy was in a depressed state of mind due to the fact that she had recently lost custody of her kids. After drinking several shots of vodka, she began writing the five suicide notes that were later found in the kitchen trash can. She wrote, "Dear John, I hate you, but I really loved you. I am sorry, I am sorry. Take care of the kids. Love, Sandy."

Then, the theory goes, she went down to the basement, tossed an electrical cord over the ceiling pipe and tied a crude noose at the end. She stacked the two VCRs on the coffee table directly below, crawled on top of them and attempted suicide. But the noose didn't hold, and Sandy tumbled to the floor, smashing her head on the table. This could explain both the bruising around her neck and the blood found on the coffee table.

The theory then goes that Sandy's best friend came over to check on Sandy and found her in her inebriated state. She helped lead Sandy into the basement bathroom to clean up. They threw Sandy's bloody shirt in the hamper and wiped up the blood from the table and the floor with rags and tissues. She then helped Sandy upstairs and laid her down on the couch. She covered her with a blanket and left Sandy there with her cigarettes.

How Sandy wound up dying that night was theorized with the help of Truth in Justice, an organization dedicated to assisting in the appeals of convictions of those believed to be wrongly accused. A forensic pathologist hired by Truth in Justice, theorized that all the vodka Sandy drank put her in an alcohol-induced coma for about five to seven hours before her death. The actual cause of her death was a combination of both blood-alcohol poisoning and carbon monoxide poisoning. The cause of the fire was examined by eight different arson investigators, all of whom came to the conclusion that the fire was accidental. But no aspect of this theory made it into the courtroom. In fact, information on Sandy's attempted suicide wasn't mentioned at all, as investigators claimed it to be irrelevant to the case.

As of this writing, Paulus has dismissed any ideas that John might have been wrongfully prosecuted. "This was a homicide….To say it's an accident, that's not only preposterous, that's laughable to me." He maintains that the judge's sentence was too light; Maloney was eligible for parole in twenty-five years. Paulus says that Maloney is a "brutal killer, a cold-blooded killer."

Gerald Boyle has said that he would appeal the case immediately. On John's innocence, Boyle says: "There is no doubt in my mind that he did not commit this crime. I will go to my grave believing I am correct in my appraisal."

John is currently incarcerated at the Dodge Correctional Institution in Waupun, Wisconsin, and is eligible for parole on February 10, 2024, when he will be sixty-seven years old. Though he was convicted of the murder, his actual guilt is still questioned by many. His family maintains his innocence, and his sister has started a campaign to get John a retrial.

7

RANDY WOODFIELD

THE KILLER PACKER PLAYER

I n the 1974 NFL Draft, the Green Bay Packers recruited a man by the name of Randall Woodfield to play wide receiver. But in the end, it wasn't Woodfield's athletic ability that would give him notoriety. Instead, he came to be considered possibly one of the deadliest serial killers in American history.

Born on December 26, 1950, in the town of Salem, Oregon, Randall Woodfield's childhood was by all measures normal. Raised in a respectable middle-class family, Woodfield had two older sisters, a father who worked as a manager for Pacific Northwest Bell Telephone and a stay-at-home mother. But signs that something was off with Randall began appearing early in his life. At the young age of eleven, he was caught exposing himself to a woman. His parents, concerned, sent him to a therapist, who reassured them that it was nothing more than an adolescent exploring his sexuality. So they let it go, in the hopes that he would grow out of it.

Woodfield went on to receive good grades in high school and was instantly recognized by coaches for his natural athletic ability. It wouldn't be long before he was the star player of the Newport High School football team. But Woodfield's underlying perversion persisted. He continued to expose himself throughout his high school years and was arrested on multiple occasions for indecent exposure. His coaches, fearful of losing their star receiver, often excused Woodfield's behavior, writing it off as nothing more than a young man's lapse in impulse control. And when Woodfield turned eighteen, his juvenile criminal record was expunged.

After high school, Woodfield attended Treasure Valley Community College, later transferring to Portland State University, where he was a wide receiver for the Vikings. Woodfield's coach, Gary Hamblet, said: "He was the nicest, most gentlemanly kid I ever knew. He was quiet and polite, hardworking, and real coachable." His peers described him as "soft-spoken" and "kind of a loner." Despite his quiet and unassuming demeanor, Woodfield's crimes continued in his college years. In his first year at Treasure Valley Community College, he was arrested for suspicion of ransacking an ex-girlfriend's apartment. He was eventually released and found not guilty by a jury due to lack of evidence. And at PSU, he was arrested on multiple occasions, yet again for indecent exposure. But he was convicted only twice and received suspended sentences. Ron Stratten, the head coach at PSU, said that he never knew of those arrests until years later. "If I had known, I would have said something to interested NFL teams for sure."

In 1974, Woodfield was offered a one-year contract to play for the Green Bay Packers for a whopping $16,000 (roughly $88,000 now). The deal came loaded with incentive bonuses, such as the opportunity to earn an extra $2,000 if he caught twenty-five passes that season, and $3,000 if he caught thirty. The money enabled him to quit his job at a Portland-area Burger Chef. More important, this was confirmation to Woodfield that he was going to play in the NFL.

Portland State University students after the institution's granting of university status by the Oregon State Board of Higher Education, 1969. *Portland State University*.

Several of Woodfield's teammates at PSU later admitted to being surprised to learn that Woodfield had been selected to play for the Packers. Former PSU linebacker Bill Handsen said that Woodfield was an "athletic kid" but that his football skills weren't the best. Charles Stoudamire, a halfback on the team, described Woodfield as vain and a little lazy. "He was nice enough, but he was odd." It was also said that Woodfield was afraid of getting hit, which is a terrible trait to have as a receiver.

In June, the Packers sent him a first-class plane ticket with instructions for an airport limo pickup to take him directly to the team's training camp in De Pere, Wisconsin. But for reasons unknown, Woodfield declined the transportation and opted instead to drive out from Oregon.

In July, Woodfield was picked to be one of the rookies to compete against the Chicago Bears in a scrimmage at Lambeau Field. Afterward, Woodfield was quoted in the *Green Bay Press-Gazette*: "I'm pretty excited. I'm just really thankful for the opportunity." Woodfield survived several early cuts and reported back to his friends in Portland that he was acquainting himself well and that he felt as though he really belonged.

The Packers thought differently. Woodfield was released from the team on August 19, 1974, just before the season began. Woodfield felt that his prospects had been hindered because Green Bay was emphasizing a run game* that year, but it turned out that the team had more legitimate reasons for letting Woodfield go.

After the disappointing cut, Woodfield decided to remain in Wisconsin. He moved to Oshkosh, where he played for the semipro Manitowoc Chiefs while working as a press-brake operator. Woodfield thought that by playing nearby for the Chiefs, Packers' execs might notice him and reconsider their season lineup. His career with the Chiefs was also cut short. Despite playing well, he was dropped after just one season. No reason was given publicly as to why, but it was speculated that the cut was due to off-the-field concerns. During his time in Wisconsin, Woodfield had been involved in at least ten cases of indecent exposure. As one law enforcement officer put it, "Woodfield couldn't keep the thing in his pants."

Woodfield, having been dropped from both the Packers and the Chiefs, realized that his NFL dreams were over. He drove back to his home in Oregon, and that was when things began to escalate.

In early 1975, Portland police began to receive numerous reports of women being attacked by a man described as "athletically built, handsome,

---

* A run game is less focused on passing and more on running the ball, decreasing the need for receivers.

and armed with a knife." After demanding that a woman perform oral sex on him, he would steal her handbag or wallet and then run off. On March 5, 1975, Portland detectives set up a sting operation using female officers as decoys. That day, Woodfield attempted to rob an undercover female officer with a paring knife and was arrested.

He was charged with armed robbery, and the police conducted an extensive interview with Woodfield. He admitted to having impulse-control issues and "sexual problems." He confessed to taking steroids and speculated that this was the cause of his changed sex drive. Woodfield pled guilty to a reduced charge of second-degree robbery and was sentenced to ten years in prison. He was freed with parole in July 1979 after serving four years.

A little over a year later, on October 11, 1980, Cherie Ayers was found raped and murdered in her Portland apartment. The coroners reported that Ayers had died from blunt-force trauma and multiple stab wounds to the neck. Coincidentally, Woodfield had known Ayers since childhood and had recently reconnected with her at their ten-year high school reunion. When homicide detectives took Woodfield in for questioning, he declined to take a polygraph test. The answers he did give were said to be "evasive

Lambeau Field. *Unsplash.com. Sunil GC.*

and deceptive." In an era before reliable DNA testing, no physical evidence existed to convict him, so Woodfield was set free.

Seven weeks later, Darcey Fix, twenty-two, and Doug Altig, twenty-four, were found shot to death execution-style with a .32 revolver in Fix's Portland home. Yet again, Woodfield was found to have a connection with the murdered woman. One of Woodfield's closest friends and a teammate from PSU's track team had dated Fix. Woodfield was suspected of the crime and brought in for questioning. Once again, there was no physical evidence to connect him to the crime. DNA testing has since that time implicated Woodfield in both of these cases. They are the earliest known murders he committed.

On December 9, 1980, a man wearing a fake beard held up a gas station in Vancouver, Washington. Four nights later, in Eugene, Oregon, a man matching the same description but with what appeared to be athletic tape on his nose raided an ice cream parlor. The following night, an hour away in Albany, Oregon, a drive-in restaurant was robbed by the same man. And a week after that, in Seattle, a gunman matching the same description trapped a waitress in the restroom of a chicken restaurant, where he forced her to masturbate him.

On January 8, the gunman held up the same Vancouver gas station he had robbed about a month before, this time forcing a female attendant to expose her breast. Ten days later, on January 18, the gunman entered the Trans-American office building in Keizer, Oregon. There, he sexually abused and shot two women, Shari Hull and another woman, both twenty. Hull unfortunately died in the hospital; the other woman survived the attack.

All of these attacks happened just a few miles from Interstate 5 exits. Word of this quickly spread, and the gunman was dubbed the "I-5 Bandit" (also the "I-5 Killer"). The description of the criminal was always the same. He was an athletic man armed with a silver .32 revolver who wore a strip of athletic tape across the bridge of his nose.

On February 3, 1981, Donna Eckard, thirty-seven, and her daughter Janell Jarvis, fourteen, were found dead in their home in Mountain Gate, California, just a mile off of I-5. Both of them had been shot in the head multiple times, and forensic tests later concluded that Janell had been sodomized. Earlier that day, fifteen miles to the south in Redding, California, an eighteen-year-old girl had been kidnapped and raped after a holdup. The following day, a similar crime was reported in Yerka, California.

Ten days later, on Valentine's Day, Candee Wilson warned her eighteen-year-old daughter, Julie Reitz, who was going out for the night, to be careful, telling her that there was a dangerous person out there. Later that night,

Julie was shot and killed in their home in Beaverton, Oregon. Oddly enough, Julie actually knew Woodfield, having met him when he worked as a bouncer at the Faucet in Portland.

The I-5 Killer's downfall came at the hands of a persistent detective, Dave Kominek. Kominek worked in the sheriff's office of Marion County in Oregon. He was suspicious of Woodfield early on. He knew that Woodfield was acquainted with several of the victims and matched the physical description of the culprit given by multiple witnesses. In addition, detectives managed to obtain a pay phone call log, which revealed that Woodfield had been using phone cards within a few miles of the murders.

The woman who survived Woodfield's attack at the Trans-American offices months before, was a key witness in catching the I-5 Killer. She picked Woodfield's photo from police files, which made Woodfield an official suspect. He was brought in for interrogation and his residence searched. During the search, police found incriminating evidence, such as the same kind of athletic tape used to bind the bandit's victims and a .32 bullet in Woodfield's racquetball bag. This was enough evidence to incriminate Woodfield. On March 9, 1982, police officially charged him with the Hull murder, attempted murder and two counts of sodomy.

By March 16, numerous indictments for murder, rape, sodomy, attempted kidnapping, armed robbery and illegal possession of a firearm were coming in from various jurisdictions in Washington, Oregon and California. Woodfield employed a public defender and pled not guilty.

In the trial, the surviving victim publicly identified Woodfield as the man who had shot and killed her coworker five months prior. It took the jury just three and a half hours to reach a verdict of guilty on all counts. Woodfield, thirty years old at the time, was sentenced to life in prison plus an extra ninety years. Thirty-five more years were added that December, when he was convicted by a jury in Benton County, Oregon, of sodomy and weapon charges. Despite Woodfield's suspected links with numerous homicides and countless other crimes along the I-5 corridor, other county district attorneys decided not to follow through with prosecutions. As Woodfield would almost certainly die in prison following the charges already received, additional trials would only drain time and resources and put the victims' families through unnecessary and painful ordeals. In the unlikely event that Woodfield was granted a parole hearing, further indictments would be pursued.

Woodfield is thought to have murdered about forty-four women, most within an eight-month period from 1980 to 1981. Now seventy years old, he is presently still serving his sentence with no chance of parole.

8

THE FURNACE MURDER OF STURGEON BAY

This story takes place in the tiny town of Sturgeon Bay, located forty miles north of Green Bay. Lying next to the Door Peninsula, the town's heritage is rooted in the water, and it's known for being a bass-fishing town. But that would change when the town was suddenly thrust into national news with a crime so heinous and ugly that it would go down in history.

It starts with Sadie Cody. Born Sadie Marsh in Sheboygan, Wisconsin, Sadie came from humble beginnings, her family being farmers. Soon after her birth, her father moved the family to Oshkosh, Wisconsin, where Sadie would grow up. After graduating high school, she pursued a career in teaching, doing so for several years in the Oshkosh area. In 1887, she accepted a higher-paying teaching position in Sturgeon Bay, which paid about $40 a month (roughly $2,833 today). She met her future husband in Sturgeon Bay, a wealthy lawyer, banker and landowner by the name of Richard Cody. The following year, in the summer of 1888, the two were married, and Sadie quit her teaching position to become a stay-at-home wife. In April 1889, she gave birth to their only child, a daughter named Irene. Life was full of promise for Sadie as she began to form the family she had always dreamed of.

Tragically, this dream life did not last long. The downfall began with the death of her husband on March 4, 1908, from throat cancer. Only four years later, Irene passed away from tuberculosis at the age of twenty-three. Lonely and vulnerable, Sadie married a local doctor named Elmer Robb just a year after her daughter's passing. Friends of Sadie tried to warn her against

Aerial view of Sturgeon Bay, Wisconsin, on a postcard published in 1908 or earlier. *A.C. Bosselman Co., New York City.*

marrying Robb, as the two had been dating for only a short period before getting engaged, and they didn't trust Robb's intentions. Despite this, the two were wed. The marriage lasted just three years. Sadie officially filed for divorce in August 1916 after finding out that Elmer had embezzled almost all of her life savings.

Four years later, she tried her hand at love one more time, marrying a traveling salesman named C.J. Kersten on December 4, 1920. This marriage lasted for three months, ending with C.J. skipping town. C.J., believing Sadie was rich due to her still living in her mansion, married her for money. After he found out that Sadie had lost almost all of her money, he bailed. In the wake of C.J.'s disappearance, the only source of income for Sadie was the two rental units she owned. One of the units happened to be leased to a man named William Drews.

William Drews was born in 1896 in the town of Wittenberg, Wisconsin. He also came from a family of farmers, but he didn't have the same opportunity of education as Sadie had. He dropped out of school at the age of fourteen to work alongside his two brothers on the family farm. Drews stayed on the farm until he was thirty-one, when he married a woman by the name of Margaret Long. Margaret and William went on to have three children together: a daughter, Audrey, in 1931; a son, Roger, in 1933 (who died of convulsions at four months old); and another daughter, Patsy, in 1940.

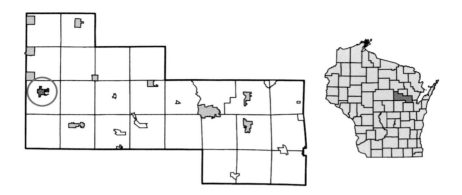

Wittenberg, Wisconsin. *DemocraticLuntz*.

In 1942, William moved his family from Wittenberg to Sturgeon Bay, where he worked building warships at the local shipyard. But when the war was over, so was his job. William then moved on to work at a local gas and oil company, where he delivered to homes and businesses. This lasted for a brief time; William was fired after being caught stealing money from the company.

On March 19, 1946, while driving to a dance at the local Odd Fellows lodge, William and Margaret were involved in a serious automobile accident. The car was engulfed in flames, and sadly, Margaret perished in the fire. William managed to walk away from the accident with no life-threatening injuries.

What he did walk away with instead was defamatory town gossip. At the time, it was a well-known fact that William was having an affair with a woman named Julia Smith, despite his claim that she was nothing more than a family friend. This led to speculation that William had murdered his wife so he could be with Julia, staging a car accident to cover his tracks. Despite the rumors, no charges were ever filed against him for Margaret's death.

Two years after Margaret's passing, William and Julia were engaged. They both happened to be renting separate apartments in the same building—the two units owned by Sadie Cody. Two days before the wedding, on April 2, 1948, William drove up to Sadie's house in the hopes of extending his rent payment. He had been fired from his job a few months before (he had been once again caught stealing from the company) and was in dire straits financially. Sadie refused.

Blinded by anger, William struck Sadie on the left side of her head, hitting her so hard that she was knocked unconscious instantly. Fearing that he would face assault charges, William quickly devised a plan. He picked up the unconscious Sadie, brought her to the basement and stuffed her body headfirst into the thirty-by-thirty-inch furnace. Then he turned on the furnace stoker switch and opened the draft, which allowed more oxygen to enter and the body to burn faster.

As he carried Sadie down to the basement, William scraped his hand against the stone wall, causing his hand to bleed profusely and leaving a blood trail everywhere he went. So he went back upstairs and looked in the first-floor bathroom for a bandage. Unable to find one, he resorted to clumsily wrapping his wound with a shower cap. He also grabbed a rag, which he used in an inept attempt to clean up the blood. He then returned to the basement to discard the rag in the furnace and checked once more to make sure it was still burning. Before exiting the house, William looked through Cody's purse for any spare cash. He stole an envelope containing $150 in rent money, which he used to pay for the cost of his wedding the following day.

William left Sadie's house that day in the hopes that people would simply assume Sadie was out of town visiting friends and that no one would notice her suspicious absence. But the next day, April 3, the townspeople began to notice a nauseating, foul odor in the air that seemed to be coming from Sadie's house. At first, people theorized that a squirrel had fallen down her chimney, causing the sickening smell. The truth was much more disturbing.

Loretta Burk, a neighbor and friend of Sadie's, frequently saw Sadie hanging out on her porch, and the two would often make pleasant conversation. Noticing the unusual lack of activity at Sadie's house, Burk called the police. Entering the home, the two responding officers immediately noticed that everything was covered in a thick layer of black dust. This was later discovered to be the soot of Sadie Cody's remains.

The first inspection of the house didn't trigger any suspicion of foul play. One of the police officers, Joseph Antonissen, actually went down to the basement and noticed the terrible odor coming from within the furnace. He opened the furnace door to inspect the smell but did not notice the remains lying inside.

Despite the initial inspection failing to notice anything out of the ordinary, Loretta was convinced that something was off. The next day, after still seeing no activity from Sadie, she called the local sheriff, Hallie Rowe, and informed him of her concerns. Sheriff Rowe decided to conduct his own investigation. He noticed something that the responding officers had somehow missed: a bloody shower cap resting near the basement furnace. Becoming suspicious, he opened the furnace and sifted through the ashes. There, Rowe discovered the skull and several bones of Sadie Cody.

When the news of Cody's murder broke, mass hysteria swept through the small town of Sturgeon Bay. Within a few hours, the local hardware stores sold out of both guns and padlocks. Thankfully, the investigation lasted just a short period. Sheriff Rowe knew that one of Sadie's tenants was William, and Rowe decided to start the investigation with him. After five hours of questioning, William broke down and confessed to the murder.

The trial began on Tuesday morning, April 20, 1948. William Drews's attorney was Frank Weis, who advised him to plead guilty of any charge short of first-degree murder. Drews rejected this advice.

At the trial, a doctor named John Muehlhauser testified that he believed Sadie Cody was still alive when she was stuffed into the furnace. Dr. Samuel Pessin, the pathologist on the case, agreed and noted how Ms. Cody's arms were positioned as though she were shielding her face from the intense flames. In addition to this, coal had been found resting on top of the body, suggesting that William had "stoked the flames." An air vent was also discovered to be open, in an attempt to increase the fire's heat, implying that the goal was total incineration.

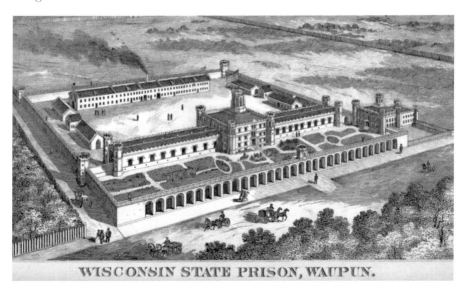

Illustration of the Waupun State Prison, 1885. Wisconsin Blue Book.

It took just sixty-eight minutes for the jury of eight men and two women to convict William Drews of first-degree murder. On Thursday morning, April 22, 1948, Judge Edward DuQuaine sentenced William to life in prison. After serving eleven years at Waupun State Prison, William applied for parole in 1959 but was denied. With his incarceration, William's two daughters ended communication with him. They visited him just once, before he died of kidney failure in 1968.

THE MYSTERIOUS DEATH OF MARGARET DREWS

Coincidentally, Margaret Drews, William's ex-wife, died in a similar manner to Sadie Cody, having been incinerated by the flames resulting from the car accident. Sadie's death brought into question what really happened the night of Margaret's death all those years ago.

On the night of Margaret's passing, a responding police officer reported finding William Drews near the scene in an apparent daze. The severity of his injuries were unclear, but he was hospitalized for about five days. William told the police that he and his wife had left their home about 9:40 p.m. to attend a dance at the local Odd Fellows lodge. At 9:45 p.m., five minutes after departing their house, the rear tire of the car blew out. William lost control, and the car went speeding into the woods, where it crashed in a grove of trees. He claimed that both he and his wife were rendered unconscious.

Margaret Drews died in 1946, but it was twenty-five months before an official inquiry into her death began. Allegedly, William admitted to killing his wife to Sheriff Rowe the same day he admitted to the murder of Sadie Cody, but no charges were brought against him for Margaret's death.

9

TOM MONFILS

SUICIDE OR MURDER?

Tom Monfils was known to his friends and family as a nice guy and a hard worker, dedicated to his job at the James River Paper Mill. But on November 22, 1992, he was found dead at the bottom of a pulp vat at the very place he worked, a fifty-pound weight tied to his neck. The horrific circumstances of his death shook Green Bay to its core and left people questioning, even today, if it was a suicide or a murder.

The trouble started on November 10, 1992. Tom Monfils made a phone call to the Green Bay Police Department. He informed them that a coworker, Keith Kutska, was going to steal sixteen feet of scrap wire cable from the mill, which, he claimed, Kutska would conceal in a duffel bag. Employees of James River were allowed to take home scrap material, such as the scrap wire cable Kutska was allegedly planning to steal. But they were required to first obtain a scrap material pass; otherwise it would be considered theft. If Kutska would have taken the time during his workday to request one of these passes, all future problems might have been avoided.

Police relayed this message to the James River Paper Mill security guards. When one security guard spotted Kutska with his duffel bag, he approached him and asked to see what was inside. He asked three times, but each time Kutska refused to open the bag, saying he was in a hurry to get home because his wife needed his car. He managed to leave work that day without revealing the contents of his bag.

But when Kutska returned to work the next day, he was immediately escorted to a disciplinary review meeting. When confronted, Kutska flatly denied taking the wire cable. Regardless, Kutska was suspended without pay for five days—not for theft, but for disobeying the security guard's orders. It was at this meeting that Kutska learned that a fellow employee had been the one to report him to the police. Kutska left the meeting angry, seeking revenge and determined to find out which of his peers had snitched on him.

Kutska returned to work triumphant. He loudly boasted to his coworkers that he had called the police department and in a few days was going to receive a copy of the taped call. Then he would know who ratted him out. Monfils overheard this and grew fearful of the potential ramifications of Kutska receiving the tape. He called the police department a total of five times and the district attorney's office an additional three times, pleading with them not to give the tape to Kutska. Jim Taylor, the deputy chief of the Green Bay Police Department, reassured Monfils that it would not be released. But due to a lack of communication in the police department, the tape was released to Kutska on November 20, 1992. Later, when the department was questioned as to why they would give the taped conversation away, the GBPD said that under Wisconsin state law, the tape was public information. Therefore Kutska (and any citizen who asked) was entitled to it. Tom Monfil's mother, Joan Monfils, later petitioned against this law, and it is thanks to her diligence that the law was annulled, making all police calls anonymous.

If this tape had never been released, who knows what could have been avoided, and whether or not Tom would still be with us today. Unfortunately, Kutska did receive the tape and subsequently went forward with enacting his idea of revenge.

The next day, Saturday, November 21, Kutska arrived at the mill at 5:00 a.m., two hours earlier than his scheduled starting time. This was in part because a coworker wanted to go deer hunting, so Kutska came in early to relieve him of his shift. But mainly, he had arrived early so that he could play the tape out loud to any coworkers who would listen. For the next two hours, Kutska carried around a cassette player and played the recording over and over to his fellow employees.

Monfils clocked in for his shift a few minutes after 7:00 a.m. He made his way to the soundproof control room and sat down with the intention of reading a newspaper. Not long after, Kutska entered the room, and it was there that he finally confronted Monfils about the call. Two other employees were in attendance for this much-anticipated altercation, Randy Lepak and Michael Piaskowski. After Kutska entered the room, he set the cassette player down in front of him and yelled out to Piaskowski, "Hey Pie-oot-ski, you'll never guess the name of this tune!" He then played the tape.

After several minutes of letting the tape run, Kutska asked Monfils if it was his voice on the tape. Feeling cornered, Monfils admitted that it was indeed his voice. Kutska then asked Monfils why he had done it. Monfils said that he had a stake in the company and a future to be concerned about. For the next several minutes, Kutska relayed his displeasure toward Monfils, finally concluding with the statement, "This is just malicious." With that, he left the control room.

Lepak and Piaskowski remained in the room and expressed their own dismay over Monfils's actions. Piaskowski said, "I can't fucking believe you would do that Tom, we're friends, we're family here, we don't do those kinds of things to each other." Piaskowski left the room, leaving Lepak with the final word. Lepak said: "You coulda cost Kutska his job. What a chicken shit thing to do. You're just lucky it wasn't me, or I'd fucking killed you." Lepak then exited the room, leaving Monfils alone.

At around 7:30 a.m., Monfils left the control room to do a turnover.* It was the last time anyone saw him alive. At 7:45 a.m., Monfils was reported missing. His coworkers suspected that the confrontation had upset him so much that he left work without notice. But when they checked his locker, they found that his street clothes were still inside. His car was still in the parking lot; Monfils had to be somewhere nearby.

It took thirty-six hours of searching before Monfils was discovered. That Sunday night, a James River Paper Mill employee looked down into a tiled pulp vat, and there she found the gruesome remains of Monfils's body. Such vats are meant to hold paper pulp until it is ready to be sent to machines to become tissue. These vats have a propeller at the base to churn the pulp and water, similar to the function of a kitchen blender. Monfils had fallen directly into this propeller.

When Monfils's body was recovered, it was discovered that a fifty-pound weight† was attached to his neck with a jump rope he had brought to the mill to exercise with on his work breaks. The autopsy showed that Tom Monfils had died from suffocation and strangulation. This led to speculation of foul play.

The investigation into the death of Tom Monfils was led by Detective Randy Winkler and took 841 days to complete. Its conclusion led to the

---

* A procedure that involves taking a full roll of paper off a machine and starting a new one.

† Such weights were common at the paper mill, as they were often used to balance older machines.

conviction for murder of not one, not two, but six of Monfils's coworkers, dubbed the "Monfils Six."

These convictions largely depended on two key witnesses, Brian Kellner and David Weiner. Brian testified and signed a written statement that claimed Kutska had performed a full reenactment of the murder at the Fox Den Tavern in Oconto County. Allegedly, this happened over the 1994 Fourth of July weekend, a full year and a half after Tom Monfils's death. Kutska and his wife; Brian Kellner and his wife, Verna; as well as the owners of the tavern, were all there and were supposedly roped into playing a part in the reenactment. According to Kellner, each person played a role as one of the six convicted men and demonstrated how the men had cornered Monfils by a bubbler, intimidated him, beat him and proceeded to throw him in the vat.

David Weiner also testified against the Monfils Six. He claimed to have seen fellow employees Michael Johnson and Dale Basten bent over, carrying something with substantial weight toward the pulp vat at 7:40 a.m. the day Monfils disappeared. Both Basten and Johnson were among those charged on homicide counts.

There was just one problem with the trial. Both of the key witnesses lied.

Years after the trial, Kellner, dying of cancer and on his deathbed, confessed that the story was entirely made up, concocted by the lead detective, Winkler. Kellner said that he signed the witness statement only because Winkler threatened Kellner's loss of custody of his kids and of his job if he didn't sign. The other witnesses in the story—the owners of the bar and Kutska's wife—also denied that any such reenactment had ever happened.

As for David Weiner, he also turned out to be an uncredible source. When David testified in the Monfils case, he was actually in prison for killing his brother during a heated argument. Five inmates at the Oshkosh prison where he was being held came forward and said that Weiner admitted to killing Monfils because he hated snitches. Even more damning, before Monfils's death was publicly declared a homicide, workers discovered a potential suicide note from Monfils. The note was found scribbled in a phone book in the small breakroom. On the front of the phone book, someone had written "page 152." Circled on that page was Tom Monfils's telephone listing, and in the margin was written, "I do not fear death, for in death we seek life eternal." But this handwriting did not match Tom Monfils's; it matched David Weiner's. Weiner confessed to writing the note to his fellow inmates. He said he did so to throw off police. But no further investigation into this was conducted.

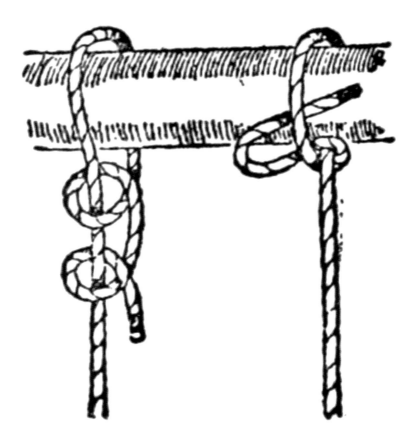

A two half-hitch knot. Scouting for Girls, *1918*.

As for Detective Randy Winkler, in 1997, he received a suspension letter from Police Chief James Lewis. The letter demanded that Winkler either resign or face being fired. By late 1997, Winkler had gone on disability retirement due to post-traumatic stress disorder and severe depression brought on by his work in the Monfils case. Though the exact reasons for Winkler's resignation are not known, it should be noted that most "resign or be terminated" letters are brief, only a sentence or two. Winkler's was twenty-six pages long.

The main speculation among his coworkers was that Monfils committed suicide. Over the years, Monfils had told them bizarre stories from his Coast Guard days, when he helped to retrieve bodies from the water. He spoke of the things suicidal people attached to their necks to make them sink faster, such as car bumpers, flywheels and heavy engine parts. When Monfils's body was recovered, a weight was found tied around his neck with a jump rope. A two half-hitch knot was used, one commonly employed in the Coast Guard. Tom's brother even stated that this knot was one Tom used to tie. All of this information was dismissed by Detective Winkler, however.

Coworkers theorized that Monfils had grown seriously stressed that morning from the intense pressure put on him by Kutska and the other employees—so stressed that he might have been triggered into doing something drastic. Tom's brother Cal said he also thought his death may have been a suicide, as Tom had struggled with depression in the past. Again, this information was not brought up in the trial.

As for the convicted men, each experienced different fates. Mike Piaskowski had his conviction overturned in 2001, due to insufficient evidence. The other men were not as fortunate. Many were not granted parole until more than fifteen years later. The first was Dale Basten, who was granted parole in 2017 due to declining health. He passed away in 2018. Basten was to be released on parole in December of that year. Rey Moore and Michael Johnson were granted parole in the summer of 2019. Keith Kutska, the supposed leader of the Monfils Six, is still in prison as of this writing. He was denied parole in 2021. All six men maintained their innocence.

The Monfils case has become notorious to the people of Green Bay and still sparks debates on the legitimacy of the trial and the true fate of Tom Monfils, despite it being over thirty years since his tragic passing.

10

WILLIAM MINAHAN'S HEAD STOLEN

The 1980s are remembered as a time of excess—drugs, heavy drinking, corporate greed and irresponsible spending driven by the increased use of credit cards. But amid all the scandals was a growing concern about the occult practice of Satanism. This concern, appropriately called the "Satanic Panic," stemmed from the fact that rituals seemed to be on the rise, specifically among the youth. The hysteria was only further propagated by the media. Talk-show personality Geraldo Rivera aired a two-hour special, *Devil Worship*, that claimed to expose Satan's underground. It warned viewers that Satanist organizations were spreading their message to the young through heavy metal music, with bands such as Ozzy Osbourne, Judas Priest, AC/DC and Mötley Crüe accused of using "Satanic" lyrics and imagery to indoctrinate the young into the movement.

The Satanic Panic finally reached Green Bay in 1987, starting with the theft of someone's head.

The head in question belonged to Dr. William Minahan. Minahan was born over a century before, on April 20, 1867, in Calumet, Wisconsin. Like his two brothers before him, Dr. Robert E. Minahan and Dr. John R. Minahan, William put himself through college and graduated with a medical arts degree. He went on to practice medicine in the city of Fond du Lac, Wisconsin. There, he met his future wife, Lilian Mae Thorpe, at a party at a mutual friend's house.

After many years of tireless dedication to his profession, Dr. William Minahan built a reputation in the community as a superior physician and surgeon. And among his friends and family, he was known as a workaholic. At the encouragement of both his wife and his sister, Daisy Minahan, William was finally coerced into taking a much-needed and much-deserved vacation. It ended up being the first and last vacation of his adult life.

The vacation in question involved traveling overseas to visit several European countries, including Ireland, the birthplace of Minahan's parents. But even on vacation, poor Dr. Minahan was unable to escape the practice of medicine. While visiting France, Daisy became deathly ill and required an emergency appendectomy, which Minahan performed. Daisy thankfully came out of the operation OK, but the family's vacation was delayed. They stayed in France to give Daisy time to heal.

When Daisy was fully rested, they continued on to their final stop, England. But because of the delay, their trip back to the United States needed to be rescheduled. Thankfully, they managed to find a trip back with the famous cruise line White Star, on the brand-new and highly esteemed *Titanic*.

This was exciting news for the trio. At the time, the *Titanic* was hailed as the shining example of the future of cruise ships. Its reinforced, steel-ribbed hull was guaranteed to be unsinkable, a boast that would go down in history as tragically wrong. After hitting an iceberg, the *Titanic* sank in the icy waters of the North Atlantic on April 15, 1912.

Because the ship was considered unsinkable, a limited number of lifeboats were available. Only 704 of the 2,200 passengers and crew members survived. Minahan would not be one of them. His last reported words were to his wife and sister as they were being lowered into a lifeboat: "Be brave."

Dr. William Minahan's remains were among the two hundred bodies hauled from the frigid water. Even though he had lived and worked in Fond du Lac, at his brother Robert's request, William's body was brought back to Green Bay and buried alongside his parents' graves in Woodland Cemetery. Later, it was moved into a mausoleum that his wife had constructed, one that overlooked the Fox River.

Interestingly, it seems that Dr. William Minahan may have had a premonition of his fate. Before departure, he had gone to see a psychic medium. This psychic warned him not to go, telling William that he would not survive the journey. Even though William did not heed the warning, it seems that the medium's claim may have affected him, as William did purchase two insurance policies before departing. One was a $100,000 life insurance policy, of which his wife was the beneficiary. The other was a $60,000 accidental insurance policy, of which his mother was beneficiary.

Right: Portrait of Dr. William Minahan. Fond du Lac Commonwealth Reporter, Gavin Bell, UK. *Encyclopedia Titanica*.

Below: William and Lilian Minahan. *Jeanne Biebel*.

Now, let's get to the head stealing! On August 28, 1987, more than seventy years since Minahan's death, a Woodland Cemetery official found that William's mausoleum had been vandalized and the crypt broken into. On inspection, it was discovered that Minahan's skull had been removed and stolen.

The next morning, the *Stevens Point Journal* published a story with the headline, "Skull Stolen from Minahan Crypt in Allouez." In the article, Brown County sheriff Leon Pieschek stated that the rest of Minahan's remains had been taken into custody by the Brown County coroner, Genie Williams, for safekeeping, as well as to ensure that no other body parts were

Portrait of Ida Daisy Minahan. *Gavin Bell, UK.* Encyclopedia Titanica.

stolen. Pieschek also said that other cities in Wisconsin were noticing an increase in grave robbing, which he attributed to the rise in cult rituals at the time. Such rituals frequently involved the use of human remains, especially skulls.

While this may have been the case with Minahan's skull, Pieschek also said that the thievery could be attributed to the "current public interest" in the *Titanic*. At the time, some artifacts had recently been retrieved by divers, rejuvenating people's curiosity in the tragedy. Or, Pieschek said, it could be neither of those two cases—just a strange, random act of vandalism.

Sergeant Kenneth Bougie, a sheriff's department investigator, theorized that the break-in of the mausoleum had occurred late Thursday night, August 27. After entry, the individual or individuals proceeded to kick in the marble face of the crypt, where Minahan's body was. The front end of the coffin was then torn off and the head removed. Bougie stated that the most notable piece of evidence found at the scene were tennis shoe prints leading up to and away from the burial site.

Three days after the theft, the skull was finally retrieved, on Sunday, August 30. Officers received a tip from a man who claimed that he overheard two youths bragging about the crime and showing off a piece of the skull. Officers managed to track down and question one of the two juveniles. After being approached by the police, the teen confessed to the crime. The second juvenile was brought into the police by his own father.

Both parts of the skull were recovered. One part was found in a vacant lot on the southwest side of Green Bay. The remainder was found in a bushy

William Minahen's mausoleum. *Evan Freiss.*

area near the mausoleum. The two teenagers in question received a light sentence for the crime. Brown County district attorney John Zakowski was quoted as saying: "The two suspects will not be waived into adult court. Even though it is a disgusting incident, the proper forum is in the juvenile system." This was also because, as Zakowski said, one of the youths had no prior convictions, and the other had a reported drinking problem that could be treated properly in the juvenile system.

Zakowski also dispelled the rumors that this was a deliberate, premeditated act with underlying sinister motives. Rather, he said, "You had two kids who were drunk, and on the spur of the moment, decided to enter a tomb." Minahan's skull and body were later cremated and given to his living descendants. Hopefully, Dr. William Minahan can finally rest in peace, instead of in pieces.

11

JOHN S. FARRELL

A TRAGEDY

T his story involves a man who was greatly loved, well respected and a trusted friend to many. Unfortunately, sometimes a single choice can destroy a life.

John Farrell was born on May 4, 1880, on Elmore Street in the city of Fort Howard (today known as Green Bay's west side). He was one of nine children born to Richard Farrell and Margaret Maher-Farrell, who were both pioneer residents and farmers in their communities. Growing up, Farrell attended his local public and parochial schools while also working on the family farm. At the age of nineteen, he left the farm to begin working at the Northwestern Railroad, where he was employed at the railyards and the downtown stations. Not long after, he left Northwestern to accept a higher-paying position as a foreman with the C. Reiss Coal Company. He remained with this company for several years.

While employed as a foreman, Farrell decided he wanted to try his hand at local politics. After a competitive run, he was elected alderman on the city council and served in this position for a full decade (1905–15). Then, in 1916, he served an additional two years as an elected official for the city commission. Farrell then spent a few years as secretary-treasurer for the Northern Transportation Company, but he returned to public service in February 1923. This time, he was appointed postmaster of Green Bay by President Warren G. Harding. He remained in this position for nearly thirteen and a half years, being reappointed by Presidents Calvin Coolidge and Herbert Hoover.

Bird's-eye view of Fort Howard and Green Bay, 1867. *A. Ruger; Chicago Lithographing Co.*

During his time as postmaster, Farrell bore witness to several historic civic events. He was in office when airmail service was inaugurated to Green Bay. He was also in office when 250,000 Wisconsin tercentenary postage stamps were sold on the first day. When he left his job at the post office after many years of dedicated service, and with the encouragement of his friends and family, he ran for the Eighth Congressional District in 1936. He easily won the Republican nomination but lost the election to the incumbent, George J. Schneider of Grand Chute, Wisconsin.

Despite his losing, Farrell's friends and family encouraged him to run for mayor of Green Bay the following spring. After a tireless campaign, Farrell wound up winning the election by a majority of nearly two thousand votes. But he held office just three days short of eleven months before tragic events cut his tenure short.

John Farrell had been appointed executor for the will of a close friend and neighbor, Mary Ann Devoye. In her will, her personal property, which consisted of cash, bonds and mortgages totaling approximately $9,000, was left to her daughter, Louisa Mart, with the provision that it should not be paid until fifteen years after Mary Ann's passing. Farrell was directed to take charge of the estate until the fifteen-year period elapsed and was required to file annual financial reports. To the spring of 1935, the executor reports were filed regularly, with the last one showing the value of the estate at about $9,000. But in 1936, the filing date passed, and the attorney of the estate, Mike Davis, received no such report. Farrell was requested several times to make his report, and when he failed to do so for over a year, County Judge Carlton Merrill advised Davis to proceed at once in securing an accounting.

Farrell was scheduled to appear in court to explain his noncompliance and to make a plea as to why he should remain executor of the fund. The date was set for 10:00 a.m. on Tuesday, March 15, 1938. But Farrell never showed up. Attorney Davis called his office but was informed that he was out. About the time he was supposed to be in court, Farrell sent his secretary, Katherine Terry, on an errand to have his eyeglasses fixed. Terry returned to the office and found Farrell gone, so she assumed that he went out to attend to some business. When he hadn't returned by 5:00 p.m., she grew nervous and eventually called the police.

Police inspector H.J. Bero arrived at the building. He tried the door to the mayor's personal washroom and found it locked from the inside. After gaining entry to the washroom through an outside window, Bero came upon the mayor's body slumped against the washroom's door. Beneath the body was Farrell's double-barreled 12-gauge shotgun, a weapon he had claimed he brought to City Hall in the event of a holdup during tax collection.

The cause of death was revealed to be suicide. Later, a handwritten suicide note from Farrell was discovered and made public in the *Green Bay Press-Gazette*. It was addressed to "Mike" (Mike Davis) and revealed the reasoning behind Farrell's failure to file his yearly reports. It read as follows:

> *This job and my troubles have driven me crazy. There is only one way out. Thank you and Judge Merrill. I bless you both with my dying breath. Mike, I am not a coward. I never took a dishonest cent in my life. Mrs. Devoye never intended to have me bonded. I saved her money for her by persuading her not to make certain investments. She wanted to do something for me.*
>
> *Mike, the foundation for this is, I paid kidnappers $8,500 [about $166,944 today] when at P.O. in 1935. Made threat of death [here, the words are crossed out and unreadable]. I have paid $2,500 to estate since then.*
>
> *God, Mike, this is awful. My wife, my family. What is life anyway? Kicking, backbiting, chiseling. A man trying to be square in public office is driven crazy by the so-called Christian people. My insurance will cover the*

shortage. Ask the surety company to be charitable. I paid them for thirteen years. If only Hank Boland* were here, he would—

There, the letter ends abruptly.

Strangely, in the three years between the withdrawal of the money and this letter, Farrell had not once mentioned to his friends, family or the authorities this supposed kidnapping threat, leading many to believe there was no such threat. What actually happened to the money Farrell took is still a mystery. He was not known to be a gambler, and he drew a good salary and lived relatively within his means. There were no external financial pressures to warrant such an action, at least none that anyone in his life could determine.

Despite this tragic end and scandal, Farrell was a well-liked member of the community of Green Bay, made evident by the thousands of people who attended his funeral. The eulogy described Farrell as having a natural inclination to take interest in people and possessing friends from all walks of life. He was said to be an all-around friendly, good-natured and easy-to-talk-to guy. If not for the strange circumstances of his death, he may have been remembered as one of the greatest mayors to serve Green Bay.

_____

* A bonding company agent who had died some time ago.

12
MARGARET ANDERSON

Note: This chapter includes a graphic description of sexual assault that may be troubling to some readers.

On the frigid morning of December 27, 1983, James Sumnicht, a local truck driver, came across a truly haunting scene.

It was 3:01 a.m., and Sumnicht had just finished delivering his load of cattle to the Packerland Meat Packing Plant, located on Lime Kiln Road on the southeast side of Green Bay. He was headed next to perform the unpleasant task of cleaning the manure from his trailer. But as Sumnicht made his way to the manure pits, located directly across from the meat plant, he noticed a shadowy figure staggering slowly out of the pit and coming straight toward his truck. The figure's long, straight hair obscured their face and made it hard to identify anything about them. Sumnicht, creeped out by this, decided against cleaning out his trailer. He thought there might be more people waiting inside the pit, and he didn't want to take the risk of coming into contact with a group of potentially drunk or crazy people.

As Sumnicht drove away from the figure, who was now hovering by the side of the road, he received a CB call from fellow truck driver Michael Brisky, who was making his way to the plant to deliver his own load of cattle.

"How's it look up there?" Brisky asked.

Sumnicht, still rattled by the experience, replied: "There's a freak across the railroad tracks. I was going to clean out my trailer, but I changed my mind fast."

Brisky was puzzled by this response but decided to continue traveling to the plant. As he approached the entrance driveway to the Packerland plant, he noticed a body lying face down on the road, blood spilling from beneath it. Brisky immediately stopped his truck, jumped out and ran to the plant's guard shack. He told the security guard to call the police.

Officers Mike McKeough and Bill Resch were the first to respond. They were on duty only four minutes from the site. When they arrived, they noticed a woman on the ground flailing her arms frantically and kicking her legs up and down. They initially thought she had been hit by a car. Resch rushed over to the woman and grabbed her arms in an effort to calm her down. But up close, he noticed how bad her condition was. Her hair was matted with snow and blood, and she had been beaten so severely that both of her eyes were swollen shut. Most notable, her neck had a six-inch cut across it and her windpipe had been severed.

The officers quickly covered the woman with a shock blanket and held down her arms in an attempt to prevent any more blood loss. But there wasn't much more they could do for so severe a wound. The woman, later identified as Margaret Anderson, passed away on that cold, dark street that early morning. She took her final breath at 3:31 a.m.

Margaret Caroline Anderson was born on October 6, 1948. She was the youngest of her five siblings born to Charlie and Mary Copple. Her parents divorced when she was very young and went on to live separate lives. Margaret spent most of her childhood with her mother in Malta, Montana, a small town of two thousand people. Despite this living arrangement, Margaret did see her father quite a bit, as her mother invited him over to the house regularly. But he was invited only when he wasn't drinking. He struggled with alcoholism, which was the reason behind the divorce.

Both of Margaret's parents were known to be hard workers. Her father worked as a sheep farmer, and her mother ran her own restaurant, appropriately named Mary's Café. Margaret proved to be just as hard a worker. From the time she was a little girl, Margaret could be spotted waiting tables at her mother's establishment. She began waiting tables at such a young age that she had to stand on crates just to be able to see over the counter. The sight of her running around with her crate and taking orders became an endearing characteristic of the restaurant, and many customers stopped in just to see her.

When she was seventeen, Margaret accompanied her friend to nearby Glasgow Air Force Base. It was there that Margaret met her future husband, Senior Airman Bob Anderson (Andy Bob to his friends). It didn't take long for Margaret to become enamored of the helicopter pilot and his fun-loving, larger-than-life personality. Despite the disapproval of her parents, Margaret dropped out of school and married Bob on November 20, 1965. The couple had their first child on September 4, 1966.

After Bob completed his commitment to the air force, the family moved to his home state, Wisconsin, and settled in the city of Green Bay. Despite initially approving of the idea, Margaret found that living in Green Bay was less than ideal. She was young, with a baby, and Green Bay was a big city compared to Malta. Every day, she grew lonelier and more homesick.

By the late 1970s, Margaret and Bob's marriage had begun to deteriorate. By 1981, they were divorced. But Margaret decided to stay in Green Bay with her child. Still the hard worker she always had been, Margaret began to work a variety of jobs. Most notable of these jobs was her employment at the Hydrant Lounge, where members of the outlaw motorcycle club the Drifters were known to frequent. It was there that Margaret became familiar with several members of the club. She became particularly good friends with a member named Terry Apfel (nicknamed "The Weasel" because of his height—five feet, four inches—and his somewhat awkward appearance).

On Monday, December 26, 1983, Terry "Weasel" Apfel stopped by Margaret's house to visit. Margaret's only son was at his dad's house for Christmas, so Margaret had the day to herself.

By this time, Margaret and Apfel had been friends for a couple of years and had been extra familiar with each other on several occasions. So Apfel visiting Margaret that day wasn't an unusual occurrence. The two decided

Hydrant Lounge as it stands today. *Evan Freiss*.

to go out for drinks and a movie. They started the evening at the Surf Club Two, a favorite hangout of Margaret's, as it was only a short walk from her house. After a quick beer or two, they headed over to the Stadium Cinema, a multiplex located near Lambeau Field, and caught the 7:15 p.m. showing of *Uncommon Valor*, a Vietnam War movie.

After the movie, they headed back to the Surf Club Two for more drinks. The bartender was quoted as saying that it seemed like Apfel and Margaret were having a good time and enjoying each other's company. At around 11:00 p.m., Apfel suggested the two head over to a bar called the Back Forty, located at 618 Bodart Street.

This bar, owned by a fellow Drifter, Mark "Shotgun" Lukensmeyer, was considered to be a "biker bar." Even though Margaret had been there on several occasions and had grown familiar with a few of the Drifters, she was still considered an outsider and not a part of the biker crowd.

The night went on fine for a little while, but problems arose when one of the Drifters' girlfriends and Margaret started fighting. The two began slinging insults and names at each other, and then the argument escalated. After the fight, Apfel got the sense that he and Margaret were no longer welcome at the bar. They decided it was time to leave.

But Margaret wasn't done. Still angry from the fight and with the alcohol fueling her, she turned on Apfel and argued with him. At one point, she pulled at his hair and slapped him across the face. Growing annoyed by her, he threw her to the ground and kicked her repeatedly. After several hard kicks to Margaret's head and body, Apfel picked her up and shoved her toward three members of the D.C. Eagles, another outlaw biker club.

"Here, you guys can have her," he said, and got in his car and drove away.

The three members in question were Randolph "Gargoyle" Whiting, Denice "Bobber" Stumpner and Mark "A.D." Hinton. Though the D.C. Eagles and the Drifters often socialized with one another, they were very separate clubs politically. The Drifters were Green Bay and northeastern Wisconsin men who liked to ride and party. The D.C. Eagles was based in the Fox Valley area and was considered a much rougher gang that could be very intimidating. The Drifters generally held normal jobs, but the D.C. Eagles made their income through drug dealing and providing muscle for local sex-industry establishments. Needless to say, Margaret Anderson had been callously thrown into the hands of dangerous people.

The three D.C. Eagles wasted no time in taking advantage of Margaret's weakened state. They began to beat and kick her. Mark Lukensmeyer, a Drifter and the owner of the Back Forty, stood back and watched the scene from the doorway. The bartender grew intensely disturbed by the violence.

Where the old Back Forty once stood. *Evan Freiss.*

She said she could hear the cracking of Margaret's ribs as one of the D.C. Eagles stomped on her. At one point, she stepped in to intervene, but Lukensmeyer scolded her. With little empathy, he warned her that she could be next if she didn't watch herself. As disturbing as the scene was, it wasn't uncommon for bikers to physically abuse and assault women. Heeding Lukensmeyer's warning, she got in her car and left.

The next two hours turned into a horrific nightmare for Margaret. While inside the Back Forty, she was subjected to truly horrendous sexual and physical abuse at the hands of Whiting, Stumpner and Hinton. Whiting allegedly hit her repeatedly with a cue stick, smacking her so hard that it snapped in half. Hinton also used a cue stick, this time to shove a cue ball into Margaret's genitalia.

Through all of this, Margaret attempted to fight back. At one point, she kicked Stumpner in the groin and then snatched Whiting's buck knife to cut Stumpner across the stomach. But she was unsuccessful, and it only resulted in more retaliation on the part of the D.C. Eagles.

At 3:00 a.m., the three men and the bar owner decided it was time to leave, and they brought Margaret with them. They pushed her into the back seat of Lukensmeyer's Grand Torino, which had been parked in the back alley. Lukensmeyer then drove down Main Street, turning right onto Lime Kiln Road. He headed to the Packerland plant and parked in the rear of the company's manure clean-out area.

Whiting exited the vehicle, pulling Margaret out by her hair. He dragged her to the back left corner of the pit area. When they reached the two-foot concrete retaining wall, Whiting pushed Margaret over and dragged her another six feet through the snow. It was at this time that Whiting pulled out his buck knife and slit Margaret's throat.

When Whiting got back into the Grand Torino, no one asked him what had happened to Margaret. Lukensmeyer drove away from the scene. He later claimed that he was unaware of what Whiting had done.

When Margaret Anderson's body was examined by a St. Vincent Hospital pathologist, it was recorded that there were eighty-nine separate injuries to the skin surface, including bruises, cuts and scrapes. The slash to the neck had severed both the airway and the vocal cord, and the external jugular vein was cut, along with two fairly large veins that ran down the front of the neck and numerous smaller arteries. All of this contributed to her death from loss of blood. In addition to this, she had suffered a compound fracture to her nasal bone. Both cheeks, the upper and lower lips and her chin had bruises covering the entire surface. Her face was so swollen that even her ex-husband had a hard time recognizing her and struggled to identify her body.

Margaret Anderson's funeral took place on January 3, 1984.

Whiting was on the run for eight months. He changed his appearance in an attempt to escape authorities. But he was eventually found on March 21, 1985, and charged with first-degree murder. Lukensmeyer received a fifty-year sentence for aiding and abetting aggravated assault, kidnapping and first-degree sexual assault. Hinton also received a fifty-year sentence. It took four and a half years to find Stumpner. Then, after his face was broadcast on *America's Most Wanted*, it took just three days to locate him. Unlike Whiting, Stumpner hadn't changed his appearance at all. He was found taking care of horses on a ranch near Golden, Colorado.

Whiting claimed to have found religion in 1995 while serving his life term. He went on to write more than a dozen religious pieces for *Between the Bars*, a blog established for prison inmates. In one of the more recent posts, written in April 2013, he claimed to be "no longer the person who committed murder. People can choose to continue to hate me for the person I was 30 years ago, but that person is already dead." He stated that he "unfortunately" cannot undo any of the pain he caused in the past, but he can "honor God and life by giving him my adoration daily." He offered no direct apology to Margaret Anderson or to her surviving family. Margaret Anderson's niece and one of the last of Anderson's immediate family, said: "There has never been any remorse. These guys didn't care. They never once contacted family members to say, 'I apologize, I was drunk, I was really drugged up.'"

At the time of this writing, all of the men have been paroled and are free. Hinton, Denice and Mark were paroled before 2012. Whiting, the only one of the four men to be convicted of Margaret Anderson's murder, was paroled in 2020.

13

TELLTALE HEART

Guilt can manifest itself in many forms. It can seep into our subconscious and disturb our dreams. Sometimes, it can even reveal the truth against our will. This chapter is the story of two brothers, a heinous murder and some telltale hearts.

It all began on August 2, 1987. Brothers Robert and David Bintz had been drinking heavily throughout the day, making their way through a case of beer they purchased at the Good Times Tavern, located at what is now 1332 South Broadway Street. As they drank, David thought about the fourteen dollars they paid for the beer (about thirty-three dollars today) and began to believe they had been unfairly overcharged. The more they drank, the angrier the two brothers got. David eventually became so worked up over this that he called the tavern in a rage. He threatened to blow up the establishment if he was not compensated for being "shortchanged." The bartender, a woman by the name of Sandra Lison, became annoyed with the accusations of the drunken caller and promptly hung up.

This only made David angrier. In a state of drunken fervor, the brothers devised a plan. They would rob the tavern that night at closing time and take the money that was rightfully theirs—maybe a little more, for payback.

As Sandra closed up the tavern that night, Robert and David ambushed her. She was the only one there, so nobody was around to intervene or call the police. During the robbery, Sandra was brutally beaten and strangled. She later died of her injuries. The two drove her body to Oconto County's Machickanee Forest, where they left it alongside a horse trail.

The body was discovered the next day, August 3. With little evidence for investigators to go on, the case remained unsolved for thirteen years. In the end, Robert and David's downfall came by their own hands.

In 1998, while serving a ten-year sentence at the Oshkosh Correctional Institution (for an unrelated charge of sexual assault against a child), David began to have frequent nightmares. His cellmate, Gary Swendby, testified that these nightmares happened nearly every night. Supposedly, David would sit up straight in his bed and scream: "Bob, kill her! Kill her! Make sure she's dead!" This was so disturbing to Swendby that he requested to be moved to a different cell, which he was denied. Eventually, Swendby summoned enough courage to ask Bintz what these dreams were about.

Bintz confessed that he'd been having these nightmares ever since he and his brother Bobby murdered a woman in a Green Bay bar in 1987. He told Swendby that they had beaten her and struck her numerous times in the face and stomach before strangling her to death. David even indicated where they brought the body, stating they had dumped her in "a forest up north." Bintz boasted how the two were confident they would never be caught because they had left behind no prints or evidence and the car they used to transport Sandra's body had been crushed years ago.

The next day, Swendby told the prison's unit supervisor about Bintz's confession. The supervisor reported this to the Green Bay Police Department. Robert Hagcund, a Green Bay police detective at the time, was the one to confront Bintz about the statement. He asked Bintz if Swendby's claim was true. Bintz bluntly replied that, yes, it was true. At a later stage of the case, David retracted his statement and claimed that his brother committed the murder and that he had nothing to do with it.

Following this confession, David was brought to trial. Two other witnesses relayed their experiences with David and his nightmares. An inmate validated Swendby's claim. He stated that he had also heard Bintz scream out in his sleep: "Kill the bitch! I told you, kill the bitch!" He also said that David had once threatened to kill him during a game of dominoes. When he started to win the game, David grew furious and proclaimed, "I killed before and got away with it." Another inmate testified that David frequently boasted to him about how he and Bobby once robbed a tavern of a couple grand, killed the bartender and got away scot-free.

A key witness for the defense was a psychologist from Appleton, Wisconsin. He testified that dreams do not necessarily mean that a person is reliving an event that occurred in real life. He said, "Dreams may mean something or may not, depending on the individual." He testified that David was "mildly retarded," functioning at a fourth-grade level, and suffered from anxiety disorder. Both of these factors made him susceptible to psychological pressures. For example, the doctor stated, during a police interrogation, David might comply and give the answers expected of him, not necessarily the ones that are reliable or truthful. Despite this defense, David Bintz was found guilty by a jury and convicted of being party to first-degree murder. He was sentenced to life in prison in May 2000.

Robert Bintz's guilt manifested itself in a different way. An ex-friend of Robert's, recounted in court an incident that had happened during the Christmas season of 1998. She recalled that she, Robert and another friend had gone up to the Machickanee Forest to cut down a Christmas tree. While there, Robert began to violently twitch and convulse. He suffered from Tourette Syndrome, but the two had never seen it manifested so severely.

Later that year, perhaps as a result of this incident, Robert confessed to her murder. She was driving Robert to visit his mother in Steven's Point, and during the car ride, he gave her the details of that heinous night. He even said that while they were transporting the body, he felt a slight movement in the back seat. To be sure that Sandra Lison was dead, he strangled her lifeless body.

Robert Bintz wound up waiving his rights to a jury trial. The reasoning behind this was his Tourette Syndrome. He was afraid that he wouldn't be able to contain his convulsions and that the jurors would be influenced by his condition. County Judge Donald Zuidmolder presided over the trial in which Bintz was convicted of being party to first-degree murder. He was sentenced to life in prison in July 2000.

Robert made an attempt to combat the decision. He argued that his conviction should be overturned because the judge wrongfully allowed for prosecutors to use statements by his brother and his brother's former fellow inmates as evidence against him. In addition, Swendby's testimony from the first trial was used against Robert, despite the fact that by the time Robert went on trial, Swendby had died in a car accident. Robert claimed that this denied him his constitutional right to confront his accusers. But the Third District Court of Appeals unanimously rejected the appeal and upheld the ruling.

Despite the sentence of life in prison, the judge had no discretion in setting parole eligibility. This means that the Bintz brothers will be up for parole after serving just thirteen years in prison. It is still largely unclear if they will ever be granted parole.

Sandra Lison's daughter spoke at the trial about how her mother was "more than only a bartender, but somebody's friend, cousin, niece, sister, daughter, and mother.…She made sure her daughters learned to ride bikes and take dance and music lessons. She bought us candy bars from the bar. She would sing me to sleep with her voice. Taking her life stole a piece of love. She won't be there when I get married, she won't be there to hold her granddaughter or grandson." Sandra's daughter said that she hopes the two brothers will come to realize how many lives they destroyed as they serve their life sentences.

14

RON RICKMAN

A STORY MADE FOR HOLLYWOOD

T he story told in this chapter is strange because, unlike other cases of homicide, it involves a conviction made only on the basis of circumstantial evidence. It completely redefined the procedures for a murder trial.

Ron Rickman wasn't from Green Bay originally. He was born on February 18, 1939, in the town of Wisconsin Rapids, an hour west of Green Bay. Not much is known about his childhood and adolescence, but Ron was thrust into the public eye at the young age of twenty-three in 1962. The reason? He had committed his first confirmed act of murder.

A father and son, sixty-year-old Frank and thirty-seven-year-old Robert Wesley, were chopping wood for pulp in a Portage County forest. Rickman approached the two with a .22-caliber rifle and fatally shot them both, Robert through his left cheek and Frank in the back. Neither survived the attack. It was later determined that an estimated forty to sixty dollars was stolen from their wallets. A Wisconsin Rapids hunter, Edward Brown, found the body of Robert, who was lying in a pool of his own blood. At first, authorities were unsure if Robert had been shot or if he was the victim of an auto accident. But after attempts to reach Frank came up empty, suspicions of foul play grew, and a seventeen-man search party was organized and dispatched. Shortly before 10:00 p.m. that night, they found the body of Frank slumped over the chainsaw he had been working with.

Rickman was later brought in for questioning. He claimed that he was shooting cans for target practice in the woods and had accidentally hit them. He later retracted this statement and confessed to killing them because he

NORTHERN WISCONSIN HOSPITAL FOR THE INSANE,
NEAR OSHKOSH, WIS.

A drawing of the original structure of Winnebago Mental Health Institute, 1885. Wisconsin Blue Book.

needed money for a car payment. Despite his admission of guilt, Rickman did not stand trial for the killings. He was ruled not guilty by reason of mental disease or defect. Doctors testified that Rickman was susceptible to psychomotor epilepsy due to a head injury he received in 1956 in a car crash. The doctors said it was likely that Rickman suffered such an attack during the time of the slaying.

Rickman was housed at the Central State Mental Hospital in Waupon until August 1972, when he was released to a halfway house in Green Bay. After his release, Rickman married a woman named Yvonne, and the two moved in together.

For many years after, Rickman lived a productive and normal life. In fact, he was involved in numerous community activities and even won an award for his work with adolescents. He was known by the teenagers he worked with as "Uncle Ronnie" and was relatively well liked. But brewing beneath his seemingly normal disposition was a dangerous murderer with a need to kill again.

It was August 14, 1981. Yvonne, forty-eight at the time, was on a shopping trip in Appleton, Wisconsin, thirty miles south of Green Bay. She would never be seen again. What really happened to her is still a mystery, as no body or murder weapon has been found. But ten years later, in 1991, Ron Rickman was convicted of Yvonne's murder.

The investigation started seven years after Yvonne's disappearance, in 1989, when a former friend of Rickman's informed police that Rickman illegally possessed a shotgun. Rickman was arrested and convicted of this minor offense.

While in jail, Rickman began to talk to a fellow inmate about what happened the day of his wife's disappearance. According to his testimony, Ron said that during the Appleton shopping trip he became angry with Yvonne and slapped her across the face. Moments later, the fight escalating, they both reached for the gun Rickman kept underneath the front seat. According to the inmate, Rickman said that "she went for it, and he went for it, and the next thing he knew, he was at home. He was smiling about it." Ron also told him that he felt the same way about his wife's disappearance that he did about the loggers he had killed in 1962. Rickman showed little remorse for either event, even making jokes about them.

The inmate's testimony allowed for prosecutors to introduce information about the 1962 murders of the Wesleys into Rickman's trial. Under normal circumstances, this would have been prohibited, due to the potential effect such information would have on the jury's impartiality. This also allowed for Robert Wesley's daughter (fifteen months old at the time of her father's death) to testify at the hearing. She said that justice had not been served against Rickman twenty-eight years earlier, when he killed her father and grandfather. "He took the life of my father. I always wondered what he would have thought of how I turned out. It's not very nice to have to learn about your father secondhand," she said.

The introduction of the Wesley case into the trial had a definite effect on people's judgment of Ron. Yvonne's brother even said that he believed Ron to be innocent until he had heard about Ron's sinister past. Ron and Yvonne's daughter even testified against him. She spoke of her memory of the day her mother disappeared. "At first, I didn't believe it, because she liked to play hide and seek with me. So when I got home, I looked behind closed doors and in closets. And when I couldn't find her, I went into my room and cried myself to sleep." She also testified that she had never seen her parents fighting and never heard her mother talk about leaving the family, so the disappearance came as a shock.

Rickman did not plead guilty. He testified that the couple had gone to Appleton so that Rickman could appear in Outagamie County Circuit Court on a worthless check charge while his wife went to shop for school clothes for their daughter. He claimed that after their fight, Yvonne told him she had to "get [her] head on straight," then grabbed two sports bags and left the car. He drove around the corner and parked, then returned to the spot where she had exited, but she had already vanished. He said he just could not understand why his wife of almost eight years would do such a thing. He maintained that he did nothing to hurt Yvonne. While no one has reported seeing or hearing from Yvonne since that day, Ron stated that he received three phone calls from her within three weeks of her disappearance.

It also came out at this time that Rickman had had inappropriate sexual contact with a minor in a youth group that he advised. He denied this as well.

Rickman's testimony indicated that, despite tension created by financial problems, there had been no talk of divorce or separation between Ron and Yvonne. But numerous witnesses said the couple had a rocky marriage and that Ron talked often about divorce. But others said they were a happy couple and that Yvonne Rickman never mentioned marital problems.

The jury took just ninety minutes to reach a verdict. Neither Yvonne's body nor any murder weapon was ever found, but Ron Rickman was convicted of first-degree homicide. Judge Richard Greenwood sentenced Ron to a mandatory term of life imprisonment. An appeals court reaffirmed this decision in June 1993. This was the second time a bodyless murder trial was conducted in Wisconsin, the first time being two years prior, in 1989, when Dane County prosecutors charged Stoughton businessman Gary Homberg with killing his wife, Ruth.

The case received lots of attention for the unusual circumstances of Rickman's conviction. In 1994, Ron's life and the disappearance of his wife were the subject of a CBS TV movie, *The Disappearance of Vonnie*, starring Ann Jillian (of the 1980s TV show *It's a Living*) and Joe Penny (of the 1980s TV show *Jake and the Fatman*).

Ron Rickman died of natural causes at the Red Granite Correctional Institution on Tuesday, February 17, 2004, one day before his sixty-fifth birthday. While Rickman more than likely was responsible for his wife's death, his conviction without any concrete evidence certainly is unnerving to hear.

15

A TALE OF EXTORTION

William Cannard was a middle-aged family man who worked as superintendent at the Green Bay West Paper Company. On Christmas Eve in 1928, as Cannard was celebrating the holidays with his wife and two kids, he received a menacing letter in the mail. The letter demanded that he pay the sender $1,000 (roughly $15,700 today) by 9:00 p.m. on New Year's Eve. If he refused, he would be shot. It instructed him to deliver the money to a location east of the city off Highway 78. The money was to be placed in a wooden box on which would be three white lights forming a triangle with a red light in the middle.

At first, Cannard took the letter to be nothing more than a strange prank, so he decided not to inform the police. He did not comply with the demand and instead continued to live his life as he always did, going to work every day.

New Year's Eve came and went and proved to be uneventful. But on the following Saturday, January 7, 1929, another letter arrived in Cannard's mail, yet again asking for the $1,000. This time, the blackmailer wanted the money delivered within two days instead of a week, or else he would be shot. Cannard finally told his wife and kids of the threat, and with their encouragement, he went to the police with the letters that same day.

At the police department, Cannard met with Detective August "Gus" Delloye and Lieutenant Martin Burke. Later, Police Chief Thomas Hawley also became involved in the case, and the three devised a plan to catch Cannard's blackmailer. They decided to create a fake "drop." Cannard would place a bag of pretend cash in the blackmailer's box, as he had been instructed to do. Delloye and Burke would be hidden in the back seat of

Cannard's car. Delloye would have a sawed-off shotgun and a .32-caliber Luger, and Burke would also be armed with a .32 pistol.

In the meantime, extra police patrols were used to protect the family. The day before the drop, Cannard received three mysterious calls. They consisted of someone asking if they were speaking to Mr. Cannard, after which three taps were heard, then the person hung up. The three taps were interpreted as signifying the three points of a triangle, which connected the calls to the blackmailer.

The planned drop was supposed to be a secret—only Delloye, Burke and Hawley were to know of the plan. But word spread throughout the department, and other policemen expressed a desire to be involved. Lieutenant William Walters and Officer Oran Wall were the only men to act on their desire to take part. On the day of the drop, unbeknownst to Burke and Delloye, Walters and Wall followed Cannard's car in a pedestrian vehicle with the intention of stopping the blackmailer themselves.

The box for the money drop was located across the street from Shorty Van Dee's Soda Parlor. Cannard walked up to it, placed the fake money in the box and then drove 150 feet past the location. Afterward, Delloye got out of the vehicle and concealed himself behind some bushes and waited for the pickup.

As Wall and Walters approached the spot to wait for the pickup themselves, they noticed Delloye behind the bushes and mistook him for one of the criminals. Delloye saw the two approaching but did not recognize them as fellow officers, mistaking them for the blackmailers. Wall pointed a shotgun at Delloye and shouted at him to halt, but Delloye, still not recognizing the two, did not comply. He opened fire with his shotgun but missed both men. At this point, Wall decided to return fire with his shotgun and struck Delloye's left side.

Delloye fired back with his shotgun five more times. Walters and Wall managed to strike Delloye multiple times on his left side, leg and torso. Delloye dropped his shotgun and fired with his pistol but again missed the men. The two hit Delloye's face, but thankfully the bullets did not penetrate the skull. Hit several times and severely injured, Delloye ran to a nearby farmhouse for shelter. He forced himself inside and collapsed on the floor, near death. Wall and Walters followed the suspected criminal, but as they approached, they saw that it was their fellow officer. Burke, who had been hiding in the back seat of Cannard's car as backup, came running toward them after he heard the shotgun blasts, ready to shoot Wall and Walters in the belief that they were the blackmailers. As he approached the scene, he recognized the two and noticed that Delloye was in critical condition. Burke and Walters carried Delloye out of the farmhouse, and he was driven to St. Mary's Hospital.

A Dr. DeCork operated on Delloye's wounds. The initial operation took an hour and a half. A day later, Delloye was again operated on, this time to remove shotgun pellets from his wounds. During the one-hour procedure, 157 pellets were removed from Delloye's face and side. A third surgery took place to remove even more pellets; 20 were removed. Fortunately, Delloye lived through these potentially fatal injuries. Walters and Wall were not fired for their interference of an investigation nor for their shooting of a fellow officer, a decision made by Chief of Police Hawley and Mayor James H. McGillan.

Burke had taken with him the bait box, but no suspicious prints were found. The box had lettering on it of a local company, Grebel-Jossart Electric Company. Just as the letter described, three flashing lights were fastened to the box, forming a triangle. A red automobile taillight lens was wired to the center. Detective Burke interviewed V.E. Grebel, the owner of the electric company, about the origin of the box. Grebel explained that it had belonged to them at one time and was probably used for the re-delivering of goods over the holidays. Anybody could have used it, but it was likely someone from the area or someone who had local connections. Burke collected the names of all employees of the company and checked their backgrounds, but no additional leads were generated.

Burke also tried to get a lead through the blackmailer's letter, contacting the postal inspector's office, but no significant information was obtained. With leads going cold, the mayor offered a $100 reward for any information leading to the arrest of the blackmailer or blackmailers, but nothing ever came up.

One theory was that a police officer, Elland "Slim" Delaney, was actually one of the blackmailers. In December 1928, almost a year after the blackmailing incident, Delaney was caught and charged with the robbery of the Farmer's Exchange Bank. Delaney and three accomplices from Green Bay and De Pere had assisted in abducting Thelis Noel, a cashier at the bank, and forcing him to open the bank's vault. Ironically, Officer Oran Wall was the one to aid in the arrest of Delaney, as he and another officer discovered the nearly $12,000 in stolen currency hidden underneath an automobile seat cushion. This cash had been taken by Slim Delaney and his cohorts during the robbery. The connection was made because of the site of the robbery. It was believed that the intended recipient of the blackmail letter had actually been Cannard's brother Arthur Cannard, who worked at the Farmer's Exchange Bank as a cashier. And because of Delaney's rank in the police, he was in the perfect position to make sure that the blackmailing incident was never solved. No charges against Delaney for the blackmailing crime were ever brought.

In Waupon, a town eighty miles south of Green Bay, an identical demand of $1,000 by blackmail was asked. But it turned out not to be the work of the same blackmailers. One telling difference was that this note was handwritten, unlike the typed letter Cannard received.

The case was never solved. The physical evidence and police records were all destroyed, and all witnesses are now deceased, so it is unlikely we will ever know the true identity of the blackmailer or blackmailers.

16

JUAN NIETO AND GREGORIO MORALES

This chapter's crime is arguably one of the more vicious and malicious to have been committed in Green Bay. In August of 2003, Jessica W., twenty-six, was kidnapped, brutally choked until unconscious, raped, set on fire and left for dead in the rural community of Rockdale, located twelve miles outside of Green Bay's city limits. Thankfully when she woke up she was able to roll on the ground to put out the fire, get up and walk to find help. (She did not want her identity released in the media; Jessica W. is a pseudonym.)

Composite sketches of the two assailants were displayed on the local news in hopes of catching the criminals. A manager at the Gold Dust Dairy in Rockdale, noticed the similarity of the sketches to two of his workers who helped with the dairy's herd.

Not long after the crime was reported on the news, Morales asked the manager for some time off so that he could sell his truck and purchase a van instead. Morales gave as a reason that he wanted more room in his vehicle for his family. Within two weeks of the attack, Nieto had stopped working on the farm and had left the area. By December 2003, Morales was gone as well. The manager decided to report his two workers to the police. Investigators came out to the farm and looked at the identification documents for Nieto and Morales. But according to him, he didn't see much action from the authorities in the weeks after his tip.

In April 2004, Morales returned to town, and the manager decided to take matters into his own hands. Not long after arriving back in town, Morales was arrested for failing to pay a traffic fine. The manager collected money from Morales's friends and coworkers and bailed him out of jail.

After retrieving Morales, he took him back to the farm. On the ride back, he offered Morales a soda, which Morales accepted. Back at the farm, the men talked, and Morales left the soda bottle on a table.

He thought the bottle might have Morales's DNA and that the police might be able to use that information to incriminate Morales. After Morales went out to the farm to work, he took the bottle and locked it up, replacing it with a fresh one from the soda machine. Morales later reentered the room and drank from this second bottle before throwing it in the trash. The manager recovered this bottle as well. After he brought the bottles to the police, it was found that the DNA on the bottles matched DNA found on the victim and DNA found on a beer can at the crime scene. But by the time the DNA results were confirmed to be a match, Morales had left to go to New Mexico.

On November 13, a story about Nieto and Morales appeared on *America's Most Wanted*. Both men were arrested not long after. Nieto was arrested on December 6, 2004, in DeKalb, Georgia, where he was found living in an apartment with his brother under an alias. After his arrest, a fellow inmate testified against Nieto, saying that Nieto spoke of the attack with little remorse, even saying that if he saw Jessica again, he would run her over. He also said he was confident that he was going to get off because there was no DNA evidence to incriminate him.

Morales was arrested seven months later in New Mexico. He pleaded no contest in April 2005 to kidnapping, two accounts of sexual assault and first-degree reckless injury. Morales made his plea as part of a deal. In exchange for the dismissal of a sexual assault charge and the reduction of an attempted murder charge to a reckless injury charge, Morales's plea entailed that he give an accurate statement about what happened and a testimony against Juan Nieto at trial. DNA evidence connected Morales to the crime, but Nieto's case relied on witness testimony. At his trial, Morales testified that Nieto was the aggressor and had used lighter fluid to burn the victim; Jessica had indicated that Morales was actually the one who did this. Despite Morales lying in court, his plea deal enabled him to receive a lesser sentence of fifty years in prison. Nieto apparently harbored hatred toward Morales for this, as he believed him to be a snitch. Nieto is quoted as saying, "All rats should die."

Juan Nieto was charged with three counts of second-degree sexual assault, as well as kidnapping and attempted first-degree intentional homicide. The jury deliberated for two and a half hours and came back with a verdict of guilty. Nieto was sentenced to seventy years in prison. If it wasn't for the bravery of the victim and the aid of the manager, this case may have never been solved.

BIBLIOGRAPHY

Banisky, Sandy. "For a Mill Worker Blowing the Whistle Had Deadly Results Justice for Tom." *Baltimore Sun*, May 17, 1995.

Chicago Daily News. "Slain Widow in Furnace, Mansion Yields Vague Clues." 1948.

Chicago Sun-Times. "Minor Says It's a Clear Case of Murder." 1948.

Chippewa Herald-Telegram. "Authorities Recover Missing Skull." October 31, 1987.

Daily Tribune (Wisconsin Rapids, WI), September 27, 1994.

Green Bay Press-Gazette. "After 'A Lot of Flack' Police Shed Tears of Joy, Relief." October 29, 1995.

———. "Blackmailers Demand $1,000 From Woman." January 18, 1928.

———. "Chronology of the Case." October 29, 1995.

———. "David Bintz Convicted." July 26, 2000, 14.

———. "Detective Delloye Wounded." January 10, 1928.

———. "Emotions." October 29, 1995.

———. "Ex-Packer Draftee Jailed." October 13, 1981.

———. "Ex-Packer Faces Murder Charges." April 10, 1981.

———. "Farrell Name Has Grisly Link to Local Lore." June 12, 2003.

———. "First Degree Murder." 2000.

———. "Friends Bear Late Mayors Body into Church." March 18, 1938.

———. "How Police View Roles of the Eight Defendants." April 13, 1995.

———. "Jurors See, Hear Victim on Tape." September 29, 1995.

———. "Michael Piaskowski, Randy Lepak." April 13, 1995.

———. "Monfils Attorneys." July 2, 1997.

———. "Monfils Attorneys: City and Police, Must Accept Blame for Releasing Tape." July 2, 1997.

———. "Murder Trial." April 21, 1948.

———. "1981 Murder." July 10, 2002, 11.

———. "$100.00 Reward for Clues to Blackmailers." July 17, 1928.

———. "Others Could Face Charges." October 29, 1995.

———. "Police After Blackmailers Stage Battle." January 10, 1928.

———. "Profiles of the Defendants." April 14, 1995.

———. "Released from Hospital Det. Delloye." January 23, 1923.

———. "Robert Bintz Convicted in 13-Year Murder." July 27, 2000, 2.

———. "Second Youth Found in Minahan Skull Theft." September 10, 1987.

———. "William Drews Stands in County Court." April 8, 1948.

———. "Witness Thrilled with Arrests." April 13, 1995.

———. June 13, 1991.

Gullickson, Denis, and John Gaie. *The Monfils Conspiracy*. New York: iUniverse, 2009.

Journal Times (Racine, WI), "Juvenile Court for Skull Theft." October 3, 1987.

———. June 14, 1991.

Kenosha Evening News. "Trial for Drews Set April 20." April 9, 1948.

La Crosse (WI) Tribune. "Titanic Victims Skull Stolen." August 30, 1987.

Milwaukee Journal, 1948.

Milwaukee Sentinel. "Bones in Mansion Furnace, Rich State Widow Missing." 1948.

———. "One of Wisconsin's Deepest Murder Mysteries." 1948.

———. "Mayors Death Shocks City." March 16, 1938.

Post Crescent (Appleton, WI). "New Legal Team, Monfils Death Was Suicide." November 9, 2014.

———. "Rickman Would Have Been 65 on Wednesday." February 19, 2004.

Rowe, Harvey W., and David K. Dodd. *Furnace Murder*. Fish Creek, WI: Bay Creek Publishing, 2014.

Salt Lake Tribune. "Rich Widow's Body Found in Furnace of Mansion." April 6, 1948.

Stevens Point (WI) Journal. "Skull Stolen from Minahan Crypt in Allouez." August 29, 1987.

Weber, Frank F. *Frank F. Weber, Author* (blog). Accessed December 30, 2022. https://frankweberauthor.com/blog.

Whitcomb, Tom. "The Packers Once Drafted a Future Serial Killer." The Bozho, April 22, 2020. https://www.thebozho.com.

Wisconsin State Journal. "Furnace Slaying Trial Set April 20th." April 9, 1948.

ABOUT THE AUTHOR

T im Freiss was born in the small town of Menominee, Michigan, located just sixty miles north of Green Bay. Throughout his life, Tim has always had an interest in criminology. After graduating high school, he enlisted in the U.S. Marines and served as a military policeman. He then had a short stint working as a jailor for the Menominee County Sheriff's Department, where he came to the conclusion that policework was not for him. Even though he did not further pursue law enforcement, Tim still finds the topic of crime, and the psychology that comes with it, fascinating. Tim moved on to a career in the paranormal. Through publishing his first book, *Haunted Green Bay*, and running the local businesses Green Bay Ghost Tours and the Nightshades Paranormal Museum, he has acquired substantial knowledge of the history of the Green Bay area. He currently resides in Green Bay with his wife, Cherri, and his three kids.

Visit us at
www.historypress.com